100 ESSENTIAL TRIATHLON SESSIONS

THE DEFINITIVE TRAINING PROGRAMME FOR ALL SERIOUS TRIATHLETES

**STEVE TREW AND
DAN BULLOCK**

**FOREWORD BY
DARREN SMITH AND JODIE STIMPSON**

THE CROWOOD PRESS

First published in 2014 by
The Crowood Press Ltd
Ramsbury, Marlborough
Wiltshire SN8 2HR

www.crowood.com

British Library Cataloguing-in-Publication Data
A catalogue record for this book is available from the British Library.

ISBN 978 1 84797 672 7

Typeset by Jean Cussons Typesetting, Diss, Norfolk

Printed and bound in Singapore by Craft Print International

CONTENTS

FOREWORD

Few people inspire others for decades. Steve Trew inspired me when I was a young coach a good few years ago now, and continues to support the development of athletes and coaches alike to this day.

This book provides an insight into the accumulated knowledge of an educator at the top of his game, and will help you with the 'juggling' of the different demands of sport and life. Bravo, Steve! I took notes when I read these training suggestions and they got me thinking deeply now as it did back then! Thanks once again, coach

Darren is regarded as the number one Olympic distance triathlon coach in the world. He coached six triathletes to the 2012 London Olympic Games; Sarah Groff of USA, Anne Haug of Germany, Lisa Norden of Sweden, Kate Roberts of South Africa, Barbara Riveros Diaz of Chile, and Vicky Holland of Great Britain.

Darren Smith

During my time in triathlon, I've learned that every single training session must have meaning, purpose and aim. It's vitally important to never waste time and to make use of every single session. 'What's the reason for this session?' 'Why am I doing this?' 'What do I get out of this?' My coach always has an answer!

The sessions in this book are absolutely spot-on; there's a reason why you should be doing them, a time, and a scale so you can fit in with your level of fitness and aspirations. Great book, highly recommended!

Jodie finished runner-up in the World Triathlon Series in 2013.

Jodie Stimpson

I have been fortunate during my career to have worked with some amazing coaches as well as amazing athletes. In the coaching world, Dan Bullock is up there with the very best. His technical knowledge and analysis of stroke is superb. Dan has improved times and technique with swimmers and triathletes of all abilities from absolute beginner to World medallists. It has been a privilege to have worked alongside and learned so much from him.

Co-author Steve Trew

INTRODUCTION

Triathlon has been a huge part of my life for the last thirty years, and the changes I have seen in the sport during that time have been astounding, in particular the rapid increase in standard of performance at all levels and the massive changes in training. Back in the 1980s, triathlon was seen as a total endurance sport with little or no room for quality training.

The rate of improvement has been hugely impressive, and in long-distance triathlon, the rate of performance improvement has been even more remarkable, from that first Ironman® in 1978, won by Gordon Haller in 11hr 46min 58sec, to the current times of sub 8hr for men and the astonishing 8hr 18min for Chrissie Wellington (GB) in the women's event. This time decrease of over 33 per cent cannot be matched by any other sport.

Of course, any new sport will see tremendous changes as it reaches out to more and more competitors, and this has been reflected in training for triathlon. There have been different phases of training as 'new' (actually often old reinvented) methods have come into vogue. There has, at various times, been a different emphasis on a particular discipline.

But it's triathlon, isn't it? So every discipline is important. What is equally important is how the training for those three disciplines fits together, and how they relate and impinge upon each other.

At one time every single training session had to be a 'back to back', or 'brick'. It works for some athletes; for others it is just extremely tiring. And that's what's important: each athlete needs to ask: What training do *I need*? What works for *me*? What is going to make me a better athlete? The bottom line for us is to find the sessions that make us improve.

We hope this book will help. It contains 100 sessions that Dan and I have used over the years and which have been effective in improving performance. There are no short cuts, but knowing what works and what doesn't, and choosing the crucial sessions to make those gains, is going to save time and avoid a lot of frustration.

An essential skill for all competitive triathletes at whatever level is juggling – time, sessions and real life! Without that skill, life becomes rushed and less enjoyable.

Steve Trew

PART I
SWIMMING

CHAPTER I

SWIMMING TECHNIQUE

Effective swimming is one of the most biomechanically difficult sports to measure in terms of recognizing and calculating what is happening when it is done well. Élite swimmers can hit the same number of strokes for length after length, but there will be subtle variations in terms of the pathway that each arm revolution takes. The more stable the foundation that these movements are based on, the greater the likelihood of more similar movements being repeated.

When attending training camps with swimmers and triathletes, it is hard not to see some key patterns develop. Issues with stroke stability and key inaccuracies are always apparent time and time again as we work with adults to improve their front crawl technique. It is always rewarding to see some significant breakthroughs in terms of getting faster from performing just a few key drills. I have relied on these 'basics' for many years now, and while they are quite simple in their appearance, the essentials of technique are there. I was pleased but not surprised when I also finally found footage of some Olympians doing these same drills in their recovery swims at a top US university.

You will see that the basic extension position and torpedo drills are referred to continually throughout the fitness sessions, such is their importance. It is not a matter of drills being performed for learning and then forgotten: drills are repeated over and over again, just as a golfer will have their swing looked at from time to time and sometimes rebuilt.

The Leg Kick

It is imperative to change your approach to swim technique in order to break through to more economical swimming. Working from the legs up may seem strange, but they do cause most issues. Improving your leg kick is possibly the biggest breakthrough you can make to your front crawl stroke. A perfect leg kick with a less-than-perfect front crawl arm pull is better than a bad kick and a perfect pull/catch position. With a good leg kick the act of swimming should be less tiring.

A wetsuit will not cure a bad leg kick, and continually pulling will not help solve the issues that are slowing your full stroke front crawl. Adding fins will generally make a bad leg kick faster, but it will not stop it from tiring you out if the kick is incorrect. Wearing a band around the ankles will reduce a bad kick but not teach you what a good leg kick is.

The kick should not be engaged to the point that it is overly propulsive. We need the kick to hold the body in position, to help initiate rotation. It is not about propulsion. It is absolutely necessary to have an efficient front crawl leg kick to swim faster. The bike and run are still to come once the swim is complete, but a good front crawl leg kick will not over-tire your leg muscles.

Remember the concept of 'hiding' to maintain a streamlined position:

- Hide the toes behind the feet
- Hide the feet behind the legs
- Hide the legs behind the body
- Look forwards but do not face forwards, hide the neck behind the head
- Hide the upper shoulder behind the head, seal up the gap between the lower shoulder and chin as the lead arm extends forwards
- Hide the arm (as it extends forwards) behind the hand
- Keep the head still, unless turning to breathe

What we want to avoid is the kick being too big – that is, kicking outside the profile of the body and creating drag. The disparity between how you imagine you kick and what actually happens can be huge. Frequently when people see their video playback they are amazed to see the width and depth of their kick compared to just how small a good kick is: they cannot believe 'that's all it is!'

It is easy to see how this happens: on dry land strong leg movements do create speed, and the bigger and faster movements usually dictate big, fast returns. The skill when it comes to swimming is limiting the range of movement. The leg kick even while mechanically accurate in terms of a relatively straight movement from the hip can still be quite big.

Using the 'plank' position as well as the Pilates 'swimmer' movement will supplement and accelerate an accurate small kick. If the leg kick is likened to the movement of a pendulum, then it is easy to see how a small movement at the hip can generate such large unwanted positions down at the feet. Core exercises will add rhythm to create a good small kick, and the core strength to control it and keep it

small. It is also necessary to have flexible ankle mobility so that the feet can turn inwards and improve 'usable surface area'. Feel the big toes tapping as a constant reminder of this aspect of the kick. This will also stop the feet splaying too far apart if you maintain a fast rhythm.

If all the above fall into place and your kick mechanics improve, then the kick will add traction to the stroke (rather than propulsion). You will then stand a better chance of creating rotation around the long axis internally: the legs, core and hips generate the ability to get the upper body rotated, and it then becomes sustainable and symmetrical. The movement is repeated over and over again.

Breathing and Head Position

Often the breathing initiates and promotes rotation as the head lifts aggressively, and it is easy to assume that you are not rotating when you are not breathing. The other detrimental impact of this movement is how the arm is usually needed to help this upward movement of the head. Similarly, if the arm is pushing down, then it is not setting a good pulling position where the body should be pulled over the hand and forearm by getting the fingertips pointing to the bottom of the pool, the palm of the hand facing the wall you are swimming away from, and the forearm moving into a vertical position.

Body Position and the Torpedo Drill
Ideally we look to create the FC body positions without the arms involved, so it continually happens regardless of whether you are breathing or not – hence the torpedo drill.

- Arms by your side, front crawl legs only, head still; ideally use a central snorkel

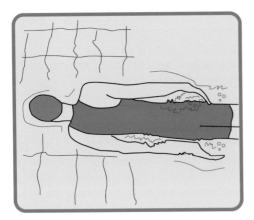

Torpedo drill.

poor streamlining and rotation, and with each breath there will be a sharp drop in speed due to the increase in surface area to your profile.

Once the shoulders start to lift above the surface from practising the drill without the arms involved, then there is a much better opportunity of making bilateral breathing a lot easier within the full stroke. The shoulders are no longer in the way – that is, low as you attempt to breathe. As the shoulders lift, the elbow is then taken higher and so the trajectory of the hands can be improved. Without rotation the shoulders are lower in the water, and in turn the elbows are kept lower as the arms recover wide.

Internal rotation means that the rotating continues even when not breathing. If the rotation originates externally from an aggressive breathing movement, from the lead arm pushing down and so not catching, coupled

- Rotate the upper body, allowing the rest of the body to follow
- Aim to bring the shoulder around to the chin alternately, do not move the chin to the shoulder. Avoid shrugging the shoulder up to the ear
- The head must remain still at all times. Using a central snorkel will allow more of this to drill to be performed without tiring

Swimming this drill for 5m from each wall with no breathing will really help. Finish the length on full stroke, and the movement of the drill will gradually enter into your full stroke.

In the torpedo position the legs are kicking, the hips rotating, and the core is involved in lifting the shoulders and getting the upper body partially on to its side. The kick needs to do this so that rotation is delivered equally and continuously. If lifting the head when breathing during full stroke drives your rotation, then it often needs a wide push down of the arm to help prop the head up. To stop this wide sweep of the arm from unbalancing you, it often needs a wide leg kick to counterbalance you. These faults will create very

A narrower hand recovery will keep the kick smaller.

An unbalanced body position needs stabilizing.

with the head lifting into the breath, swimming will become almost one-armed and the body will run the risk of injury as the shoulder takes a lot of the pressure.

The Extension Position

The role of the extension position is to help you hold the arm outstretched, and to learn to breathe off the outstretched arm without it falling away, so the head is supported when breathing.

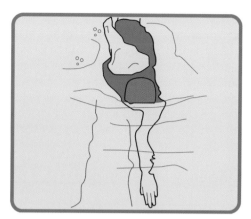

Extension position.

- The lead arm is outstretched and submerged; this should lift the trail shoulder above the surface
- As the head looks down, tuck the submerged shoulder into the chin
- The trailing arm lies along your side. The surface shoulder aims to remain still
- Initially use a snorkel to perfect the body position. Gradually dispense with the snorkel so that you can practise breathing to the side
- It is advisable to use fins initially

If the torpedo position promotes the rotation to come from within, then the extension position is the drill that teaches a leg kick that is sufficient to hold you on your side. Over-kicking will lead to a more tiring kick that is trying to work to create propulsion. If the leg kick is under control and stabilizes, then we should be able to hold the surface shoulder steady and stable in this position; if the kick is out of control then it will be reflected in vigorous movements in the surface shoulder. Extension is sometimes referred to as the 'Superman' position.

Adding a central snorkel to the full front crawl stroke will allow breathing to take care of itself. As skills are developed to perform better hand pathways under the body, there will be a reduction in the negative forces that would otherwise throw the legs around. It is important to work on the body position, leg kick and rotation before moving on to 'the catch' and 'the feel of the stroke'.

When the negatives of poor technique are removed and the body position improved, swimming speed will improve because many of the finer movements will become more intuitive. The sensation of moving forwards will become more apparent, as the front crawl stroke technique improves.

An efficient leg kick will help the upper body rotate, which will in turn allow the arms to start to engage correctly. While standing on the poolside the 'torpedo' position is quite straightforward to perform. With the feet on the floor there is a strong foundation for rotation. In the water that basic foundation is lost and we rely on the kick to recreate it. Without that, even a good arm pull (balanced and symmetrical) will suffer if it has to pull a bad leg kick through the water. The upper body and arms do most of the work and the legs far less, but it is essential that all areas work together.

Triathletes should not be able to pull (swim arms only with a pull buoy to lift the legs) faster than they can swim, but many do! Most good long distance front crawl swimmers can 'pull' long-distances at a fast speed, but it is hard work. It should be possible to swim full stroke front crawl at the same 'pull' speeds, but it should be a much easier overall effort.

Efficiency of Technique

One definition of swim efficiency is the number of strokes taken over any distance. An élite swimmer of average height may swim one length of 25m in thirteen strokes, though many triathletes will take between twenty and twenty-five strokes. Lowering the number of strokes taken will decrease the effort needed and will keep the stroke rate relaxed and efficient.

What is it that chips away at your efficiency to make it possible to reduce your distance per stroke down in the 1.20m range, rather than closer to 1.60m? If we follow all the negatives that are possible in front crawl, it is easy to see how they add up; the following are the most common mistakes:

- If you are trying to pull the body over the hand, and yet the hand is pushing water down to the bottom of the pool, then you are not going forwards
- If the fingers are wide apart, and not the 3mm ideally recommended, then the hands are going to slip under the body without the body moving forwards
- If you are facing forwards with the head up, then more drag occurs
- If through a lack of rotation both shoulders remain submerged, then you will not move forwards as easily
- Swinging the arms wide of the body on recovery and crossing the centre line on

entry means you are moving sideways, not forwards
- If a strong two-way pivot at the knee hampers your kick, you will send yourself backwards

All these mistakes in technique will limit your forward movement to well under 1.60m per stroke. Even the toes pointing to the bottom of the pool are going to hold you back and slow your progress.

A sure sign that power and strength beat technique in the short term is how most people are able to maintain the pace needed to swim 25min for 1,500m, but only for a short distance. Eventually drag increases as streamlining decreases, water is pushed in the wrong direction, more surface area than necessary is exposed, and so your length of stroke decreases and speed decreases as well.

How do we keep the stroke count low?

- **Think** – Smallest body profile through the water
- **Think** – Push every drop of water backwards towards the feet, but with as little effort as possible
- **Think** – Repeat it over and over again
- **Think** – Whole body, and not just arms

Streamline your stroke, iron out as many flaws as possible, and work on as many of these good habits as possible until they are ingrained. Continued, repeated, accurate practice will ensure that good technique becomes a habit. Have the full body contribute to your stroke to keep it as relaxed as possible. Keeping an eye on stroke count within your main sets will help check efficiency, but think of your stroke count not as an absolute minimum to strive for, but as an alarm bell sounding a warning if it goes too high in the middle of a fitness training session.

Fitness

How long should each swimming session be? A 90min key fitness session will allow 20min warm-up including drills, then a 50min main set plus a warm-down. It can be helpful not to bike or run earlier in the day ahead of a key session: resting the legs a little is critical to keep cramping at bay and avoid 'pulling' rather than swimming 'full stroke'. The mechanics of the leg kick alone are quite stressful, in particular to the calf and the arch of the foot. The quality and length of your session will improve if you can approach it slightly rested, and arrive hydrated and with some nutrition. You may be depleted from an earlier session and will need the energy. Gels tend to 'sit' better than bars, but it is quite individual and you will work out your own preference.

Your swim progress will accelerate if you make use of fins, paddles and a central snorkel. A kickboard is handy but not necessary; the extension position provides plenty of kicking practice.

Time spent learning to breathe bilaterally will even out your pull, promote symmetry in your body position, and stop any one side or arm recovery becoming too dominant. With fewer breaths taken per length, it will not be easy, so don't rush it. Most athletes breathe to one side on race day, but it is good to be able to choose which side.

The single biggest factor that will help your swim improve will be adding a session to your routine each week. The fewer days spent not in the water each week 'unlearning technique' will massively help. Aim to count your sessions per month, rather than per week, to get a more realistic idea of the amount of swimming training that you are doing.

BAD HABITS TO AVOID IN TRAINING

Don't glide into the wall.
Don't stop 2m short at the end of any repeat; that will really add up over a season. 20 × 100m becoming just 98m each time due to some congestion at the wall each swim will be worth thousands of metres missed out by the end of the year.
Keep 5sec (or more if possible) behind the swimmer in front.
Don't draft all the time in training: you will create a false sense of faster swimming, which may lead to disappointment on race day.
Do lead a slower lane. You will work harder as a result.
Do wear drag-trunks occasionally.

CHAPTER 2

TRAINING TERMINOLOGY AND EXPLANATIONS

Some triathletes just endure their swim training rather than enjoying it, and when we examine some of the main sets in their sessions then it is no surprise! Possibly this is due to the mindset that triathlon is a long and endurance-focused event, so swim training should be as well. Certainly there is a time and place for a long, steady swim to reassure yourself that you are well prepared for race day – but not every session. For many triathletes in training, long, straight swim sessions are often the main offender in that they lack originality, creativity and purpose. Swimming training sessions should be motivating, challenging and inspiring. If you feel that a training session has gone quickly, then this is a huge compliment to the coach and an indication that it has been interesting and motivating.

The Importance of Preparation

For novice adult swimmers, swimming may well seem like the high-maintenance, annoying relation to bike and run training – but with some organization and planning it needn't be. In terms of getting to the pool, the equipment needed, organizing what to do and anticipating lane space, it will need more planning than the others. But if you have the correct session prepared to take with you, and if you know the specific equipment to take, and which lane at the public pool you might be in, then the pre-session stress can be alleviated and you will accomplish more in the least amount of time necessary.

A common problem is to arrive at the pool for a session unprepared and uncoached. With all good intentions, 24 × 100m of front crawl (FC) can become twenty by the time you walk across the car park, eighteen by the time you have changed, and down to just ten by the time you have swum eight of them! But if you have your session printed out and on poolside with you, then you have some accountability and you will get more done.

Set targets, count your sessions per month, add up the distance swum, try to match or improve month on month, and you will rarely find yourself leaving the pool early.

What do we need, then, from swimming training? Time needs to be spent on fitness, speed, technique and open-water skills both in the pool and in open water at the appropriate times and as race season arrives. To remain focused and motivated, frequent test sessions should be performed to provide feedback on certain areas of your training, and to indicate how you should next focus your efforts. There is no point becoming a fitter, but slower, swimmer – and likewise there is no point having perfect technique if 1,500m of front crawl exhausts you. Perhaps the biggest open-water sin is having the fastest swim speed of the day, but inadvertently swimming 1,700m because you have been zigzagging across the 1,500m race you should have swum. If you cannot swim relatively straight through a more balanced and technically correct symmetrical FC, then you would easily be adding 300 to 400m to an Ironman® distance swim.

The following sessions should encompass a wide range of skills and allow you to arrive on race day well prepared, fit, and technically efficient and prepared for the uncertainties that swimming in open water can throw up. Swim drills either resolve bad habits or encourage good habits within your stroke, and should be practised to the best of your ability, frequently, as an ongoing part of your training. Open-water skills allow you to navigate more effectively, become accustomed to the lack of clarity, the jostling of multiple swimmers in a small area, and effectively deal with issues that otherwise might end a race for someone unprepared.

If there is one overriding factor to be considered when it comes to improving your swimming, it is performing structured and well-planned sessions on a more frequent basis. The sessions need to provide feedback, and should let you know if what you are doing is of use, and if it is correct. Otherwise swimming can be cruel, in that 'just aimlessly' swimming for a few hours per week can result in your making very little progress, because it is relatively easy to get it completely wrong. If you swim only once per week, even if the session is well planned and prepared for, you will have six days of 'unlearning' between swims, which will allow bad habits to remain. Not enough practice of any new movement will allow it to fade, and any existing incorrect movements will remain.

Once you are happy swimming your intended race distance within the fitness sessions in the pool, then ideally you will need to consider taking this fitness and technique outdoors in the very different environment

that is open water. It is rare to meet anyone who enjoys his or her first swim in the open water. Weekly attendance and practice once the weather is warm enough is simply the best advice: slowly building duration across frequency builds confidence. Adding open-water skills will enable you to negotiate more confidently all that might be thrown at you on race day.

It is possible to construct these sessions loosely into a plan of three sessions per week with the occasional test added. The fitness sessions include three main set options, so that all abilities should be able to draw something from each. If you miss an opportunity to swim a key session, then given the busy schedule that your triathlon training plan dictates, it will be difficult to make it up: with three discip-lines to consider, there is a big impact on the amount of rest and recovery you receive, and this will impact on the other two disciplines. If you are tired from biking and running it is tempting to add a pull buoy and float through a swim session. Usually rotation suffers at this point, and more stress can be put on the shoulders, especially if paddles are used. To more closely mimic full stroke, consider wearing a swimthin suit (a thin wetsuit), which will help elevate a tired body position without actually taking something away from your full stroke.

At the first signs of any aches or pains in the shoulders, immediately stop any paddle work. It would also be wise to reduce the amount of pulling you do. Add fins if you do need to take the pressure off your shoulders to finish a key session. If one shoulder starts to click or ache, then get it looked at. Also, better technique usually results in the likelihood of problems reducing, so arrange for a swim coach to check your swim technique in case something has been impinging on an area of your stroke.

The shoulder is a miracle of engineering allowing movement in all directions, and it should be looked after. If you are embarking on adding significant volume to your swim programme through these sessions, then consider a shoulder strengthening routine to enable the many small muscles to cope.

Getting the Best from your Training Sessions

To get the best from your training sessions, the following key points should be observed:

Try to arrive poolside as rested as possible, given that you are squeezing three sports into one week: it may not be easy! Tired legs from biking and running will possibly persuade you to reach for a pull buoy, and to perform a less than optimal session. You will also possibly cramp more quickly, and again this will ruin your session. Good hydration and nutrition will help, and you will sweat while you swim, so keep drinking. A lower limb dynamic stretch routine will help the body to become a little more accepting of the unaccustomed swim positions that we are asking while swimming.

Make use of swim equipment to maximize and accelerate swim improvements. The sessions will include frequent use of swim accessories, and if you are allowed to use them, you should. Fins and central snorkels seem to particularly offend pool operators.

Give swim improvements time – quite a lot of time. Swimming is more like learning a language or a musical instrument. Timing, coordination, ungainly new movements in the alien environment of water, along with restricted breathing, makes this a huge undertaking. However, given how completely wrong some movements can be performed, early adjustments can result in dramatic progress, as even

small changes away from paddling water in the wrong direction to channelling it in the correct direction will yield great improvement. The slower you are, the more you can improve with frequent swimming, whereas the better you are, the harder it becomes to achieve improvement – as with most things; although to me, even small improvements are worthwhile, even when swimming will take up only a small proportion of your race.

A pull buoy should be a part of your swim training, and you will find they are used throughout these sessions. However, they should not be a continually relied upon aspect of your swim technique. If you can pull faster than you can swim, then you should ask a coach to take a look at your leg kick and work out what is holding you back. Usually it is a combination of the toes pointing to the bottom of the pool from tight ankles/shins, or pivoting at the knee on both the upsweep and the downsweep, rather than from the hip on the upsweep.

Consider easier pure drills sessions as an ideal lower heart rate (HR) zone training session. Initially swimming full stroke front crawl may well be so inefficient that it will be quite exhausting. Many triathletes feel that they cannot swim slowly enough to get into their lowest 'aerobic' HR zone as set by their coaches. Many of the simple body position drills performed with fins and a central snorkel could be considered an easy 'active recovery' style of session and should keep the HR lower.

Add dry land movements from the worlds of Pilates and Yoga if your mobility, coordination or body awareness is poor. Many sports need a solid upper body moving in one direction. A good swimming body position needs for the head to be kept still yet the upper body to rotate from side to side through its long axis. Try this standing in front of a mirror, allowing the hips to follow the movements of the upper body. It is not easy. Likewise if you cannot point your toes away from the body a pure streamlined body position is not going to be easy to achieve, which will keep the legs sinking.

The arms and legs should not be relied upon to work as stabilizers propping up a poorly positioned body alignment or by splaying outwards preventing you from rolling on to your back. (There is more of this in the 'Technique' chapter.) One of the key technical issues is that of the swimmer pushing down with a straight arm, the palm of the hand facing the bottom of the pool to help elevate the head for a breath. Each breathing stroke then becomes inefficient. The worst case often needs a large splayed leg kick to counterbalance the wide straight arm sweeps, thereby creating more drag. There is a good reason that even Olympians still perform simple body position drills such as the 'Extension' position. When the body is balanced and the arms and legs are no longer needed as stabilizers, then they can be used far more effectively for propulsion.

Be sure of the location of any simple pivot point: often in triathlon swimming we get the location of a pivot point in the wrong place. Straight arms when submerged and bent legs are a major hindrance. The best streamlined position comes from a straighter leg, but keep in mind it is fine to bend at the knee on the downsweep but not the upsweep.

Similarly we are looking for a wide elbow pivoted to expose the forearm and palm of the hand so it is facing the wall you are swimming away from. If you pivot at the wrist or at the shoulder then you will not have both surface areas in the correct position. Faster swimming needs good streamlining and the arms channelling the water in the correct direction for best movement forwards. Look at the technology and design in the forearm panel of your wetsuit if you need convincing.

Work to reduce a high stroke count, 'high' being anything above one stroke per metre, so twenty-five strokes in a 25m pool. However, don't chase an unrealistically low score that involves excessive kicking and gliding. Make use of an optimal amount to warn you of your stroke deteriorating during longer fitness blocks of work, if the stroke count goes much above its normal range.

Many of the new swim watches offer a measure of efficiency by combining stroke count and time. These two factors when added together can be of great use, and you do not need a watch to help: just add the time taken to swim 25m to the number of strokes taken. If this total score comes down through better overall efficiency and fitness, then faster swimming is inevitable. Push too hard with a frantic stroke and while the time might come down, the stroke count will rise. Glide too much to lower the stroke count, and the swim time will go up, keeping the overall score high. Record this on a regular basis to gauge improvements to efficiency.

Aim to attend a realistic monthly number of sessions rather than a weekly amount. Fourteen sessions per month will usually ensure good progress and improvement. An aim of four sessions per week may well be admirable and may occasionally be reached, but frequently four sessions in one week will mean only two in the following week. This is not really enough to overcome bad habits, instil better technique and improve fitness. Fourteen per month allows the flexibility to try to include on a weekly basis a technical endurance drills session to be swum, which could be treated as a recovery session, an open-water skills session (in the pool), and finally one or two solid fitness blocks of work either in the pool or open water. Add in two swim test sessions at some point each month, and this will be a well-balanced approach to swim improvements. You can add these sessions to your regular weekly routine for some variety as they will stand alone, or create a small training plan to fine-tune the final few months ahead of a key race.

Swimming Terms and Jargon

The following glossary will try to offer an insight into how to read, understand and put into practice a more productive swim session. It will allow you to read and understand the accompanying sessions, and to get the best from them.

Typically a 60min swimming training session could be broken down in the way described below. These are just guidelines, however, and you will come across the following areas of a session taking many different formats depending on how you implement them into your tri training, and the training phase you are entering, and the time of year.

Prior to entering the water some simple dry land mobilizing exercises should be performed, in order to enter the water 'warm'.

Warm-up: 15 per cent: easy swimming to mobilize and encourage blood flow.

Subset: 20–25 per cent: used as an extension of the warm-up to build HR levels or to introduce some skills that need to be done while 'neurally fresh'.

Main set: 40–50 per cent: a sustained period where the HR is elevated. Ideally at least 30min.

Subset: 11–10 per cent: a secondary subset might be added to start a longer, more technical warm-down, depending on the intensity of

the main set, or often sprints will be added if appropriate to the season.

Swim-down/cool-down: 5–10 per cent.

Warm-up

The warm-up often starts on dry land prior to getting in the pool, and involves literally warming up the body ahead of intense activity. Usually it is an easy swim, predominantly front crawl or backstroke with some drills included. Swim aids such as paddles are avoided due to the increased resistance. Butterfly and breaststroke are also not usually used in the early parts of a warm-up due to the higher intensities they command.

A sample warm-up routine might be 200 FC, 150m drill (alternate 25m catch-up/fists clenched), 100m backstroke, 50m breaststroke arms with FC legs.

Subset

This is usually swum as an extension of the warm-up to build HR levels so that when the necessary speeds and HRs of the main set are asked for they can be delivered immediately. Often main sets will get faster as they progress due to the athletes becoming fully warm and able to swim at the speeds we would like to see. Depending on the time of year, the subset could also be used to introduce any swim drills or technique elements that need to be done while 'neurally fresh'. Drills done post main set are often compromised due to fatigue.

A sample subset might be 8 × 25m, rest 10, streamlined submerged FC kick to 10m, surface and build to fast full stroke.

Main Set

The main set is the part of the session that is the focus or aim of the swim training plan. Swim exercises will be performed in many ways to promote speed, endurance and/or technique. There are many training methods used to promote and develop aspects of your race, depending on the season/training phase. This is the main focus of this section.

Interval sessions

Interval training is perhaps the most familiar at your triathlon or swimming club... When attempting a session, there are several ways the efforts can be increased to help elevate your HR. Four key areas are adjustable to make the session more intense, more productive and meaningful. First, the distance of the repeats you swim – in week one, 4 × 200m, building to 4 × 300m in week four.

Then there is the interval of the swim – you get 2min to swim 100m FC on week one, before attempting another repeat. As your fitness improves you will get more rest as you swim each 100m faster; after several weeks the interval might come down to 1:50.

The number of repeats swum may also be increased, adding to the intensity of the session. Thus in week one you may only make 5 × 100m FC on your interval before reaching exhaustion, but the following week we might aim for 8 × 100 on the same interval.

The aim time is the final variable that can be manipulated. Your coach might advise 8 × 100m FC with an interval of 2min but a target of 1:45, meaning you get 15sec rest before starting again. After four repetitions at this pace the effort might be too much, and you slip to 1:50. These are the benchmark times and efforts you should bear in mind and record in a training diary. If you know your personal bests (sometimes called personal records) you will know if you are improving.

With a few weeks training hopefully you would improve and can try the 8 × 100m FC with an interval of 2min and an aim time of 1:45 again. If you make the set your coach might increase the number of repeats to twelve, or bring the interval down to 1:50 and encourage you to a target of 1:40. The possibilities of progression in training are endless.

Interval training can cover many areas, helping you to work on key aspects of your race, and helping to make your training race specific.

Speed Sessions

Training at higher speeds is often practised with very short repeats (12.5–25m) and lots of rest, and differs from maximum effort training. Swimmers will often try to swim faster than maximum speed with the use of long stretch cords pulling them through the water faster than normal. This involves a lot of pool space, however, and realistically we might have to settle for fins. Swimming short bursts with fins will have a similar effect of generating 'overspeed'. For the more serious triathlete this type of set would be useful for helping to drop an annoying drafter, or to jump back on to a pack a few metres in front.

Swimming to Heart Rate (HR)

Instead of a time-based target, if your coach is familiar with your HR zones they might challenge you to swim to HRs. Your interval could also be HR-based, leading to a set such as 8 × 100m FC with a target of 80 per cent of your maximum HR, and a resting period interval of waiting to recover down to 60 per cent of your maximum HR. This means when you have finished your 100m swim you would check your HR to ensure it was 80 per cent of your maximum, and you would check it repeatedly until it fell to 60 per cent of your maximum HR.

This style of training is highly individualized and can potentially cause some issues if done in a lane with four or more swimmers all taking different rest periods.

For the triathlete coming from a non-swimming background and unfamiliar with swim aims and sensible intervals, these types of training will probably make a lot of sense. Until you are familiar with your swim abilities you might try this approach given how familiar with zones you might be from your bike or run training.

Negative and Even Split Swims

A main set of 400m might be swum in a negative split fashion. 'Back end' endurance is your ability to finish a race strongly, and to work on this your coach might ask you to negative split each 400. This could be time-based, where you swim the first 200m in a certain time, and then swim the second 200m 10sec quicker. Alternatively the effort levels could be targeted so that the first 200m of the swim is performed at 60 per cent effort, and then the second 200m at 80 per cent effort.

Even split swims are similar in that you are simply aiming to offset the fatiguing effect by swimming the second half of a swim at the same pace as the first half. HRs will invariably go up, and a 400m swim with a target of 5min would attempt to be swum in two 2:30 sections. This way of learning pacing will carry over most effectively to race-day swim pacing. By not starting too quickly you should get on to your bike a lot fresher.

Mixing Strokes

Medley training involves swimming all four strokes usually in the sequence they are raced in competition. Thus butterfly starts the sequence, then backstroke, breaststroke, and finishing with front crawl. The ability to swim all four strokes makes training infinitely more interesting and variable. It is well worth learning the other strokes for many reasons, but in addition triathletes perform a lot of FC, thus putting a great deal of stress on the body through just one range of motion.

To mix in some of the other strokes gives the shoulders, for example, a new range of motion to help reduce the chance of injury. Backstroke is an ideal recovery stroke to unwind from too much FC motion, and overall fitness improves due to the 'cross-training' effect as you mix muscle groups. The different strokes will also need effort from different parts of the body – thus breaststroke being predominantly leg

driven will give your poor FC-ravaged shoulders a chance of some recovery! Your feel for the water when swimming FC will also improve as you channel water through new pathways creating forward momentum.

Build Swims

A build swim would involve a gradual pace and effort increase for the duration of the assigned distance. You could either do this time-based, or with effort levels, e.g. a 6 × 300m build FC, where the first 100 of the 300m should be at 60 per cent, the second at 70 per cent, and the third at 80 per cent.

Your coach could also specify a time-based build swim, where you should improve by approximately 5sec per 100m for the duration of the 300m. Despite the differing effort levels between 100s, the 300m is swum continuously; the rest period will be taken between 300s. After the first 100 you will continue straight on to the remainder of the swim. If there is a large wall-mounted clock to the side of your lanes you will be able to check your split times. A change of pace in the pool is something that many triathletes struggle with. For the more competitive age grouper this is an essential element.

Reducing (Descending) Sets

A reducing set would mean that repeat after repeat gets quicker than the previous repeat. Targets could be assigned as either time-based or effort-based. For instance: 4 × 200m FC, reduce 1 to 4 from 60 per cent to maximum. In this case the first 200m would be swum at 60 per cent effort, the next at 75 per cent, the third might be 85–90 per cent, and finally you would finish the last at maximum effort.

From a time-based point of view your coach may be able to ask for specific target times, aiming at hitting 3:40 on the first 200, 3:30 on the second, 3:20 on the third, and to finish with your best effort. A challenge might even be set, which could be to try and break 3:15.

This is a potentially competitive and challenging main set that will ensure triathletes push each other for the top spot.

Broken Swims

Broken swims form an interesting challenge. In an effort to swim faster than your race pace you could be set a broken swim where you attempt to break your best time for a distance. This is made possible by breaking it into smaller sections with additional rest — not to be confused with a rest interval: with a broken swim you would take your own short rest period at the set distance.

Thus in a 25m-length pool you might be set 3 × 200m broken with 5sec at each 50m at a sprint-distance race pace. If your best time for a pool-based 400m was 6min, then your aim would be to beat this by swimming each 50m in about 45sec. Between each 50m you would take your own 5–10sec rest, making this slightly easier. In this example the swim sections could be broken at 100m or 25m to make the challenge harder or easier.

Broken swims are particularly valuable about two weeks before major competitions to help fine-tune 'race speed'. The sets would usually be longer than the example given, and worked out for best 1,500m or Ironman® distances.

Hypoxic Training

Breath-holding while swim training is used more now to keep the head still during FC swims and to improve technique. Unnecessary or excessive head movement during FC will increase resistance and drag, affecting your ability to remain streamlined. Adopting a breathing pattern where you take a breath on alternate sides at challenging intervals (every third, fifth or seventh stroke cycle) will help to keep the head still for longer, instilling the sensation of a solid head position. Turning to breathe should be the only time your head moves.

Approach this style of training with care, as headaches can be an issue, and diminished lung capacity in older swimmers will make this very demanding. Rather than recreating high-altitude effects, reduced breathing training creates hypercapnia – more CO_2.

Using this as a technique style of training, swimmers can be challenged to perform the last 25m of a set of 100m swims by taking just three to six breaths (ability dependent). If the swimmer refocuses on streamlining and distance per stroke, small efficient leg kicks and a good catch, the O_2 requirement per stroke should come down and the breath limit will be achievable.

Time/Distance-Based Swims

A challenging alternative to swimming on an interval basis is to swim as far as you can in a given time and create challenges this way. Or you swim a set distance as fast as you can. These overall times and distances can give you useful information to then calculate average shorter swimming repeat times.

The traditional T20 is used to find out the total distance (or how many lengths) you can swim in 20min. From this, various swim speeds can be calculated and used to set repeat times. A triathlon version of the T20 involves 4min of kick, 6min of pull, and a final 10min swim for a brutal test of fitness.

One variation of time-based swimming is the 'Pyramid of Pain': this involves 1min FC, followed by 2min, 3min, 4min, 5min – all FC – where an optional 6min swim is the pinnacle. A whistle is blown at the end of each timed portion, and you then take 60sec rest. Part of the rest period is used to return to the nearest wall ready to start the next swim. We then go down in time, swimming 5, 4, 3, 2, 1min, with the attempt to swim further on the way down compared to on the way up for a challenging 30min of swimming. With a big group, half of the swimmers can start from the opposite end of the pool. For the swimmer going 'last', try not to get caught by the leader at the opposite end.

Test Set
(*See* Sessions 18–21.) A necessary part of recording and checking your progress is to test yourself on a regular basis with a bench-mark set. At an élite level the parameters would be kept identical down to the small-est detail, such as performing the test at the same time of day, in the same pool, and using a similar warm-up before the set. The test sets can take many forms, to measure differ-ent elements of your swim progress. Swimgolf is useful for efficiency and checking technique, getting a feel for an optimum stroke rate. We can also use it as a measure of performance. An 'add up' main set as described here will give an indicator of current 1500m ability. It will give confidence of making the distance for those setting out and a possible race day prediction. My variation of the traditional T20 combines three elements to mimic the nature of our sport. Improve all aspects of your FC swim and you will swim a further distance in 20 minutes. My last test set is the broken swim designed to challenge over the main race distances. Early on they will give you the confidence that the distances can be achieved and as you progress you can do them faster.

Swimgolf (sometimes called 'golf score') consists of adding the stroke count to time (in seconds) over 25 or 50m, and combin-ing the two for a score. Attempting to lower the score with inefficient speed will keep the score high. Attempting too much distance per stroke will lead to a slow time and not an opti-mum speed, keeping the score high.

Critical swim speed is a useful statistic to know based around a timed 400m and 50m swim. As this improves you can be sure your aerobic capacity is improving, among the many things it measures.

To complete a session the all-important swim-down is needed to avoid carrying tired-ness over into your next session.

Swim-down
A swim-down will aid recovery from a hard training session or race. Also known as the cool-down period, it is a sustained, easy swim of at least 3min, which is the time it takes for the heart to realize it is not needed for such hard work. It will also help bring your pulse back down and reduce the dilation of blood vessels. HR levels will decrease back to normal levels, and rates of breathing will return to normal. A training session should always finish with a 200–400m cool-down, perhaps longer depending on the intensity levels in the session.

If swim technique has deteriorated, then I would suggest perhaps paddles, fins and a central snorkel: these will help realign your swim technique and improve it. Slowly remove item by item during the easy swim until none remain. Now you will have managed to reduce the tired and poor technique that otherwise you may have been carrying into your next swim session.

I encourage some form of backstroke to unwind from the usual long FC sessions. If full backstroke is beyond you, try double arm (this reduces timing issues) with a pull buoy between the legs.

Being aware of the terminology will help you to get more out of the sessions, and to make better use of them. The language of swimming can seem a little baffling, but try not to be deterred by it. Be creative with your planning, and be aware that a good technique needs to be worked on before moving on to more serious fitness swim sessions.

CHAPTER 3

THE SWIM SESSIONS

The thirty swim sessions described in this section are divided in the following way:

Swim sessions 1 to 5: Endurance
Swim sessions 6 to 10: Rebuilding technique
Swim sessions 11 to 13: Super sets
Swim sessions 14 to 18: Technical endurance
Swim sessions 19 to 21: Swim test
Swim sessions 22 to 24: Pool-based open-water skills
Swim sessions 25 to 27: Open-water fitness
Swim sessions 28 to 30: Race taper

Making the Best Use of the Sessions

Consider the following formula to work out an idea of the number of repeats you can perform, and to make best use of your time in the pool when you start to use these sessions. Each individual will work through them as their own ability dictates. The target you set depends on your current ability. As long as you are swimming further and faster in the time you have, that is the best indicator of progress. You can 'test' on regular intervals with the appropriate test sessions included so you have an idea of how much you are improving. Some of the sessions are designed to be swum individually. Some are best swum in a group situation, since the camaraderie amongst teammates will help you through the tougher parts.

In the past it has been suggested that the novice main sets would be an ideal focus for sprint-distance triathletes, intermediate main sets for standard distance, and advanced for 3.8km competitors. This is not set in stone, as you might be a better swimmer looking for a faster 1,500m swim so could build more endurance occasionally by swimming the longer main set of the advanced session.

If you have sixty minutes available to swim, then start the session and work through it in its entirety. If you get through 75 per cent of the session, then in future where the session offers four to eight sets of a certain part of the session, you would aim for six sets. This is not an exact science, but you will get the feel for distance achievable in time, and this will give you an idea of the distance you can cope with at the moment. If possible you should further tweak the sessions so the main set is at least 30min of work for an hour session.

Counting Lengths and Pace Control

The large wall clock can help in counting the number of lengths you have swum during longer swims, if you keep on eye on it. Suppose you set yourself a swim of 400m (sixteen lengths in a 25m pool.) You might already have an idea of your best 400m time, but it is not so important if you do not. If we start on the red 0 of the large clock you find on the walls of most swimming pools, then it is helpful to check the two-length split. If we see the red 50 as we touch at 50m then if we have not gone out too hard we should be approx 1:45 (red 45) at the four-length marker.

Pace control helps, and this regular checking of time will guide you. At length six we should be seeing red 40, then red 35 for a 3min 35sec 200m split. The pattern of subtracting 10sec initially, then 5sec with each swim, will have us move anti-clockwise around the clock. If you lose track, as I usually do, at around lengths ten or twelve, then just check the clock position for an update. Sighting the red 25 tells you, providing you are swimming similar stroke counts and keeping the HR consistent, that you are highly likely to be at twelve lengths. Another four lengths and you will finish on the 15 for a 7:15 swim, fairly evenly split from the 3:35 halfway point.

The very first two lengths are generally a fraction quicker due to the more accurate streamlined push and glide, the lower fatigue being fresh and general sensation of easy speed. The key thing is to recall whether you started on the black or the red top.

Try to spread the sessions so you build volume and distance swum over several weeks, adding to the number of sessions swum. This would be ideal before resting up to consolidate improvements during a rest week, and progress before building again. The training plan can also build through the year and help you approach race season in peak shape, easing back a little, tapering off, as you approach race season. Too often we see people getting into peak shape around February or March, yet key races are not due until June or July.

Major Points

Think about quality rather than quantity when swim training. There is no point in practising drills or aiming for great technique when you are extremely fatigued, as you will gain little benefit. All drills should be practised over short distances with plenty of rest, before you start attempting longer drill sets. The technical endurance sessions are designed with this in mind, with small amounts of technique work swum at the start or end of lengths so they quickly integrate into the full stroke.

Practise any drills to the best of your ability; don't try to rush things. The longer you spend on trying to build your new stroke, the better the end product will be. Add fins, snorkel, even a thin swim wetsuit to help maintain accuracy.

When practising any drills always relate the key aspects of the drill to the swimming stroke. Equally, relate aspects of full stroke to the drills. If we swim FC with our head down (aside from breathing), then we should practise kicking in the extension position, lead arm outstretched with the head down, turning sideways to breathe, mimicking full stroke FC.

Continue to practise any drills in warm-ups and cool-downs in all sessions swum. Drills don't just get left behind once performed reasonably well, but should be a full part of your regular swim practice.

When practising any drills always concentrate on one aspect of the stroke only – this will help reduce the feeling of being overwhelmed with too many parts of the stroke to focus on. Most restrict bad habits or encourage good habits, one aspect at a time. Few work on multiple areas, but for the drills that do this, leave them until the basics have been mastered.

Some Example Swim Sessions Explained

Warm-up

1 × 800m front crawl (now referred to as FC, but also known as freestyle), every odd length breathing 3s, even lengths every 2s. Or BP3 and BP2 on alternate lengths (where BP refers to 'breathing pattern').

Here we will swim twenty-four lengths of a 33.3m pool, or thirty-two lengths of a 25m pool as a steady warm-up. Do not be afraid to mix up some drills within this swim. If you struggle to breathe to both sides, then 5m of torpedo drill off each wall before resuming full stroke FC will help (see Chapter 1). If you can lift your shoulders above the surface of the water just from using your leg kick and core, then when the arms are reintroduced it should be easier to find more time to breathe to the historically weaker side. Keep the head still, both arms by your sides, leg kick only, try to lift the shoulders, rotating from side to side.

You should concentrate on breathing every third stroke on the odd lengths and every second on the even lengths. Ideally it is nice to swap sides when BP2 is engaged perhaps halfway down the pool.

Subset

3 × 200m, building within each 200: 66m steady, 66m medium, 66m strong – or 50m steady, 100m medium and 50m strong to finish, with 45sec rest.

While still getting fully warmed up for the main set, often a subset will be swum: here pace will pick up and HR increase slightly as we continue to warm up. In a 33.3m pool the set is to swim three times six lengths (200m), with 45sec rest taken before starting the next six lengths. Each six-length swim should be increased in speed: start out with two lengths medium, then two lengths faster, finishing

with two lengths strong, or consider at 85 per cent of maximum HR.

Main Set

12 × 100m FC with 20sec rest, improve the times of the 100s in three blocks of four. How hard the fourth, eighth and twelfth 100m swims might be depends on the proximity to races and the stage of your training cycle.

So you swim faster with each 100m from one to four, five to eight and so on, and you take 20sec rest between each 100m. If you are working very hard on the last 100m swims, then you could take an extra 30sec after the fourth 100m swim before commencing the next block. During the general training season (not the race season) we will swim the 100s to 85 per cent effort as we are only taking 20sec rest between 100s.

After the main set it is important to bring the level of the HR down slowly to help relax the breathing and rest the body, otherwise we could induce muscle soreness soon after the completion of the session. The last 10–15min of each session is all about slowing down and resting. It is a gradual process, so we perform a shorter set, focusing on some good FC technique

Warm-ups, subsets and cool-downs offer the chance to work on a variety of skills that are particular to you. Some examples are given to help you build your session once you have chosen your main set from the many options that follow.

Typical Warm-Ups (25m Pool)
General:

(400–800m)
400m as 2 lengths FC, 2 lengths choice, rest 10sec between blocks of 4 lengths.
400m as 2 lengths FC, 2 lengths of a favourite drill, rest 10sec between blocks of 4 lengths.
If pushed for time, swim these as 200m swims.

Distance dependent:
100m swim, 75m pull, 50m drills, 25m kick (250m): Novice
200m swim, 150m pull, 100m drills, 50m kick (500m): Intermediate
200m swim, 200m pull, 200m drills, 200m kick (800m): Advanced

Long distance:
(600–1,000m)
400m FC, 300m choice drill, 200m choice, 100m pull, no float.
If pushed for time, drop the 400m and swim the 300m drill as FC.

Typical Subsets
Building pace:
(500m)
2 lengths easy, 3 lengths build, 4 lengths easy, 5 lengths build, 6 lengths easy.
Build swims progress from 50 to 80 per cent effort, ideally with a central snorkel.
Easy swims could include drills.
Optional fins and paddles.

Drills focus:
(400–800m)
200–400m as 1 length easy into 3 lengths build to 85 per cent, with fins and paddles. Rest 60sec.
200–400m as alternate lengths single arm FC, odd lengths left arm, even lengths right arm. Unused arm to trail by your side, attempt to breathe to the non-pulling side. Use fins if allowed.

Speed:
(200–600m)
(8–24) × 1 length, descend in blocks of 1–8, 40–80 per cent effort range, rest 10sec between each 1 length. Ideally with fins and snorkel.

Warm-Down (Cool-Down)
Typical technical FC warm-down:
(400m)
Can be swum as 50m swims if pushed for time.
100m FC with a central snorkel paddles and fins. Swim on the black line on the bottom of your lane if possible, and check the hand pathways under the body. Be as technically accurate as possible.
100m FC with a central snorkel and paddles.
100m FC with a central snorkel.
100m No swim accessories.
Remind yourself of great FC technique before finishing; rehearse taking this great FC technique into your next session. Use the swim equipment to realign the stroke if it is a little tired after any main set.

Breathing pattern work:
(300m)
1 length BP 2, 4, 6 to the left, continuous pattern, easy pace, rest 10
1 length BP 3, 5, 7 continuous pattern, rest 20
1 length BP 2, 4, 6 to the right, continuous pattern, easy pace, rest 10
1 length BP 3, 5, 7 continuous pattern, rest 20
Repeat 3 times

Other strokes:
After any particularly long FC main sets it is advisable to try some non FC if you are competent in the other strokes. Some simpler variations are possible, such as breaststroke arms with FC legs, double arm backstroke with a pull buoy, FC arms with butterfly legs; these allow some alternatives without having to learn the other strokes in full and all their intricacies. The different movements work well to help relax the shoulders and stretch them out.

SWIM SESSION 1

Session objective: Endurance 1 of 5

Teaching point
Use the easier swims for a technique review. Check length of stroke, and count the strokes
– maintain an even count as the pace increases.

Main set
Novice
(800m)
1 × the following:

500m FC, alternating 1L at 50 per cent, 1L at 70 per cent, rest 30sec (optional pull buoy)
300m FC, increase effort by 100m, at 50 per cent, 60 per cent, 70 per cent

Intermediate
(1,600m)
2 × the following:

500m FC, alternating 1L at 50 per cent, 1L at 70 per cent, rest 30sec (paddles and snorkel)
300m FC, increase effort by 100m, at 40 per cent, 60 per cent, 80 per cent
Rest 60 between the 800m blocks

Advanced
(3,200m)
4 × the following:

500m FC, alternating 1L at 50 per cent, 1L at 70 per cent, rest 30sec
(fins and snorkel on the odd 500m swims, pull on the even 500m swims)
300m FC, increase effort by 100m, at 40 per cent, 60 per cent, 80 per cent
Rest 45sec between the 800m blocks

Total distance   **800–3,200m**

SWIM SESSION 2

Session objective: Endurance 2 of 5

Teaching point
BP3.2 means take a breath after a third stroke, then a second stroke. This keeps the breathing to both sides but is not quite so taxing as pure bilateral breathing.

Main set
Novice
(800m)
8 × 100m, rest 15, swum as 1L BP every 2 to the left,
1L BP every 2 to the right, and 2L BP3.2

Intermediate
(1,000–1,600m)
(5–8) × 200m, rest 20, swum as 2L BP every 2 to the left, 2L BP every 2 to the right and 4L BP3.2

Advanced
(2,800m)
Start with the intermediate set, and then continue into:
3 × 400m, BP3 then 5 within each length for 2 lengths into BP2 for a length to the right then to the left for a length. Repeat the pattern for 400m

Total distance   **800–2,800m**

SWIM SESSION 3

Session objective: Endurance 3 of 5

Teaching point
A firmer catch and pull, coupled with a better leg kick, creates economical speed. Taking more inefficient strokes will lead to fatigue.

Main set
Novice
(800–1,200m)
(8–12) × 100m: increase effort in blocks of 4, rest 30 between each 100m, rest 60 between blocks of 4. Attempt to drop 5sec per 100m ending up at 80 per cent on Nos 4, 8, 12

Intermediate
(1,200–1,800m)
(6–9) × 200m: increase effort in blocks of 3, rest 30 between 200s, rest 60 between blocks of 3. Drop 5sec per 200, ending up at 80 per cent on Nos 3, 6, 9

Advanced
(2,800m)
7 × 400m: increase effort in blocks, 1–3 then 1–4, rest 35 between 400s, and rest 60 between blocks. Aim to drop 10sec per 400, ending up at 80 per cent on Nos 3 and 7

Total distance   **800–2,800m**

SWIM SESSION 4

Session objective: Endurance 4 of 5

Teaching point
We are looking for a good cruise speed on the pull, and then get faster on the back end
1 length swims. A good session to work on back end speed.

Main set
Novice
(1,200m)
6 × 200m swum as follows: rest 30 in between each 200m (100m FC pull at 70 per cent,
rest 10 into 4 × 1L, rest 10, getting quicker by the length)

Intermediate
(2,400m)
8 × 300m swum as follows: rest 30 in between each 300m
(200m FC at 70 per cent pull, rest 20 into 4 × 1L, rest 10, getting quicker by the length)

Advanced
(3,200m)
8 × 400m swum as follows: rest 30 in between each 400m
(300m FC pull at 70 per cent, rest 20 into 4 × 1L, rest 10 getting quicker by the length)

Total distance   **1,200–3,200m**

SWIM SESSION 5

Session objective: Endurance 5 of 5

Teaching point
Alternate every 50m the pull buoy upstairs (the traditional position between the thighs) and down (between the ankles – try to keep toes pointed) on the pull swims. Optional paddles on the FC swims.

Main set
Novice
200m FC at 65 per cent effort straight into 300m pull at 75 per cent effort. Rest 1min, and continue into:
200m FC at 75 per cent effort straight into 300m pull at 85 per cent effort.
(1,000m)

Intermediate
200m FC at 65 per cent effort straight into 300m pull at 75 per cent effort. Rest 1min, and continue into:
300m FC at 75 per cent effort straight into 400m pull at 85 per cent effort. Rest 1min, and continue into:
400m hard at 85 per cent (no pull buoy)
(1,600m)

Advanced
600m FC at 65 per cent effort, straight into 400m pull at 75 per cent effort. Rest 1min, and continue into:
600m FC at 70 per cent effort, straight into 400m pull at 80 per cent effort. Rest 1min and continue into:
600m FC at 75 per cent effort, straight into 400m pull at 85 per cent effort. Rest 1min
(3,000m)

Total distance
1,000–3,000m

SWIM SESSION 6

Session objective: Rebuilding technique 1 of 5

Teaching point
Taking something away encourages the body to compensate: we clench the fist to utilize more of the forearm.

Main set

Fist needs to be clenched but not tight. Remain relaxed.

Hand and forearm now pulling creates an effective combination.

Depending on your race distance you will perform sets of the following:
150m FC at 50 per cent effort into 50m drills, 5 strokes both fists clenched, 5 strokes normal FC and repeat the drill pattern. Rest 30
150m FC at 60 per cent effort into 50m drills, 2 strokes both fists clenched, 2 strokes normal FC and repeat the drill pattern. Rest 30
150m FC at 70 per cent effort into 50m drill as one length one fist clenched the other hand normal, into one length the other fist clenched the other hand normal. Rest 30
150m FC at 80 per cent effort into 50m drills as one length fists clenched above the water on recovery, one length fists clenched below the water. Normal hand positions at all other times. Rest 30

Novice: 1 set	800m
Intermediate: 2 sets	1,600m
Advanced: 4 sets	2,400m

Total distance   **800–2,400m**

SWIM SESSION 7

Session objective: Rebuilding technique 2 of 5

Teaching point
Slowing the stroke down allows a greater accuracy of hand pathways under the body. Alternating single arms (catch-up) is a great drill for this.

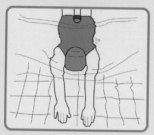

Peform ten kicks in the 'catch-up' position before taking an alternating single arm.

A wide high elbow leaving the hand under the body creates an effective pulling pathway.

Main set
Novice
4 × 200m swum as:
Odd 200m: 150m at 60 per cent pace into 50m of 10-kick catch-up.
Take 10 kicks between each arm cycle; arms remain outstretched in front during kick
Even 200m: 50m of 10-kick catch-up into 150m of FC at 75 per cent effort. Rest 30 between each 200m

Intermediate
5 × 300m swum as:
Odd 300m: 250m at 60 per cent pace into 50m of 10-kick catch-up. Take 10 kicks between each arm cycle
Even 300m: 50m of 10-kick catch-up into 250m of FC at 75 per cent effort
Rest 30 between 300m swims

Advanced
6 × 400m swum as:
Odd 400m: 350m at 60 per cent pace into 50m of 10-kick catch-up
Take 10 kicks between each arm cycle
Even 400m: 50m of 10-kick catch-up into 350m of FC at 75 per cent effort
Rest 30 between each 400m

Total distance   **800–2,400m**

SWIM SESSION 8

Session objective: Rebuilding technique 3 of 5

Teaching point
Maintain an even stroke count on this set; concentrate on an unhurried stroke. Fingertips point downwards when pulling the hand back; keep the palm of the hand facing the wall you are swimming away from.

Main set
500m FC with a breathing pattern 3/5/3/7 by lengths, repeat for the duration. Count the number of strokes taken on an early length
400m pull, with paddles and snorkel if allowed. Keep the head still
300m, no accessories, but try to maintain same stroke count as earlier
200m pull, with paddles and snorkel if allowed. Keep the head still
100m, no accessories, but try to reduce stroke count by 1 per length to refocus on good technique

Novice
(600m)
Start at the 300m. Count the number of strokes taken on an early length

Intermediate
(1,500m)
Start at the 500m and work down

Advanced
(2,500m)
Work down from the 500m, and work back up to the 400m

Total distance   **600–2,500m**

SWIM SESSION 9

Session objective: Rebuilding technique 4 of 5

Teaching point
If the 'advanced single arm' proves too much, return to the original style of drill with the non-stroking arm out in front. 'Advanced' implies the unused arm remains at the side of the body and does not move. Breathe away from the stroking arm between arm cycles. The stroking arm 'rests' out in front during the breath. The upper body fully rotates so that it more closely mimics full stroke as compared to the traditional.

Set the catch position, fingertips down, and pivot at the elbow.

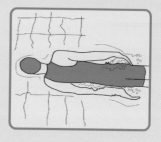

As the hand now holds the water, rotate the shoulder through to the chin.

A strong kick and hip rotation will help the arm recover.

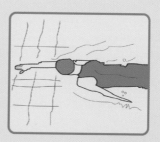

Return the stroking arm out in front and finish in the extension position.

SWIM SESSION 9
(continued)

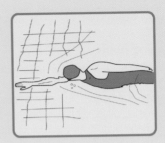

*The basic extension position needs to be good
as it creates a firm foundation for the single
arm drill.*

Main set
Novice
(800m)

8 × 100m FC, rest 20 between each swim

Odd swims: First length of each 100 should be swum as single arm (half length left, half length right). Add fins if attempting advanced single arm

Even swims: Full stroke FC, steady but technically as good as can be, taking from the previous drill where the body would have worked harder to balance itself with only one arm working

Intermediate
(1,500m)

10 × 150m FC, rest 20 between each swim

Odd swims: First 50m of each 150m should be swum as single arm (1 length left, 1 length right). Add fins if attempting advanced single arm

Even swims: Full stroke FC, steady but technically as good as can be, taking from the previous drill where the body would have worked harder to balance itself with only one arm working

Advanced
(2,400m)

12 × 200m FC, rest 20 between each swim

Odd swims: First 50m of each 200m should be swum as single arm (one length left arm, one length right arm). Add fins if attempting advanced single arm

Even swims: Full stroke FC, steady but technically as good as can be, taking from the previous drill where the body would have worked harder to balance itself with only one arm working

Total distance   800–2,400m

SWIM SESSION 10

Session objective: Rebuilding technique 5 of 5

Teaching point
Maintain good technique throughout, take more rest if you feel that your technique is falling apart. Count strokes on the 200 FC swim and rethink your technique if this number starts to go up. Work the catch-up a little more accurately on the next cycle if it does.

Main set
500m swum as follows:
50m: 10-kick catch-up, 10 kicks between each single arm cycle
200m: Pull at 70 per cent, preferably with a snorkel
250m: FC swim at 80 per cent, BP (breathing pattern) 3, 2, 3, 2 continuous for each length
35sec rest between each 500m swim

Novice
Aim for 2 × 500m

Intermediate
Aim for 3 × 500m

Advanced
Should aim for 5 × 500m

Total distance   **1,000–2,500m**

SWIM SESSION 11

The next three sessions are 'super sets' for those bank holidays or training camps when you can get a little more done.

Session objective: Super set 1 of 3

Teaching point
A dry land mobility routine (not stretching) will warm the body ahead of getting in, allowing you to get up to speed sooner. Warming the lower limbs with some ankle circling will possibly help to avoid cramp.

Main set
(1,500m)
Blocks of 5 × 300m swum as:
250m FC steady effort, straight into 50m *hard*, rest 25sec
200m FC steady effort, straight into 100m *hard* (with paddles), rest 35sec
150m FC steady effort, 150m *hard* (no swim aids, just swim!), rest 45sec
100m FC steady effort, straight into 200m *hard* (pull and paddles), rest 60sec
50m FC steady effort, straight into 250m *hard*

Novice
1 × through

Intermediate
2 × through

Advanced
3 × through

Total distance   **1,500–4,500m**

SWIM SESSION 12

Session objective: Super set 2 of 3

Teaching point
A milestone in swim circles is the legendary 100 × 100m. Build towards this via this stepping stone main set. Ideal for a mixed ability group session where camaraderie amongst team members will keep you going. If possible a 2min interval works well for two to three lanes of mixed ability, such as on a training camp.

Main set
10 swims full stroke FC
10 swims pull with optional paddles
10 swims full stroke FC
10 swims pull
10 swims full stroke FC

Novice
Attempt 50m with each swim, resting 30, or choose an interval your lane can cope with allowing at least 30sec rest

Intermediate
Attempt 75m with each swim, resting 30, or choose an interval your lane can cope with allowing at least 30sec rest

Advanced
Attempt 100m with each swim, resting 30, or choose an interval your lane can cope with allowing at least 30sec rest

Total distance
2,500–5,000m

SWIM SESSION 13

Session objective: Super set 3 of 3

Teaching point
This set can be used as an active recovery from a hard bike/run session or just a tough set. The harder way to swim this set is to start quite strong with limited rest and hold a constant average throughout. The extra awarded rest balances the fatigue build-up. Preferably you would set an interval for the first block and then add rest to it, for instance 2min on the first block, then 2:05, 2:10 and so on

Use one set as an active recovery session, two sets for the tougher format.

Main set
Novice
(1,200m)
12 × 100, swum in blocks of 4
Block 1, rest 15sec between 100m
Block 2, rest 20sec between 100m
Block 3, rest 25sec between 100m

Intermediate
(3,200m)
16 × 100, swum in blocks of 4 (1–2 sets)
Block 1, rest 10sec between 100m
Block 2, rest 15sec between 100m
Block 3, rest 20sec between 100m
Block 4, rest 25sec between 100m

Advanced
(4,000m)
20 × 100, swum in blocks of 5 (1–2 sets)
Block 1, rest 10sec between 100m
Block 2, rest 15sec between 100m
Block 3, rest 20sec between 100m
Block 4, rest 25sec between 100m

Total distance   **1,200–4,000m**

SWIM SESSION 14

Session objective: Technical endurance 1 of 4

Teaching point

There are two aspects here: integrating drills into longer FC sets for technically accurate aerobic conditioning; and using the speed of the full stroke or the wall push-off to maintain body position while a short block of drill work is done without fins.

Main set

Brams drill

Perform 3 breaststroke arm pulls with FC legs off each wall before continuing the length full stroke FC. The first part of the breaststroke arm pull is not too dissimilar to the FC 'scull into catch' that will set up a good FC hand position.

Keep the breaststroke arm pull small. Rest 45

Tri extensions

Perform four to five triceps extensions off each wall to wake up the triceps, and start to feel them contribute to the full stroke FC performed for the rest of the length. Tuck your elbows into your sides, fingertips down; palms face the wall you are swimming away from. Arms pivot 90 degrees at the elbow. Push through the back of the stroke, before returning to the start. (Keep the thumbs forwards so there is no stress on the shoulders when returning the hands to the starting position.)

Rest 45

Paddle work

Swim alternate 50s with and without a large set of paddles. Roll your fingertips over the end of the paddle. The lower part of the paddle should now cover the wrist, encouraging a full 'hand and forearm' involvement in setting your catch. No straps involved.

Rest 45

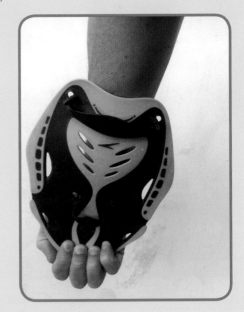

With this grip, you can quickly add or remove the paddle.

SWIM SESSION 14 (continued)

Advanced single arm
This is a tough drill that invariably needs fins and snorkel to be done well. With 5, 7 or 9 FC strokes between blocks of the single arm drill, use this speed to give you the momentum to try two complete single arms with the unused arm by your side.

Get your air on the full stroke so you can focus on the drill fully.

Rest 45

Fists drill
Swim 6 strokes normal FC, and then continue into 6 strokes with the fists clenched. This builds on the paddle work by incorporating the diminished hand shape. Alternating will set up a good FC hand position.

Rest 45

Novice
Swim each block as 150m swims

Intermediate
Swim each block as 300m swims

Advanced
Swim each block as 400m swims

Total distance   **750–2,000m**

SWIM SESSION 15

Session objective: Technical endurance 2 of 4

Teaching point
Use the breath-holding aspect of this main set to keep the intensity low and get some big metres swum. Focus on aerobic fitness and fine technique. BP = breathing pattern.

Main set
(1,500m)
500m FC swum with fins, BP5 (i.e. a breath every fifth stroke) Rest 25
400m FC, swum with paddles, BP4   Rest 25
300m FC pull, BP3   Rest 25
200m FC swim, BP2   Rest 25
100m strong, 3 breaths per length, your choice where you use them
100m easy, then repeat as follows:

100m FC, BP5   Rest 25
200m FC, BP4   Rest 25
300m FC pull, BP3   Rest 25
400m FC with paddles, BP2   Rest 25
500m FC with fins, your choice of BP, but the brave will try 5–7 per length
(In total 3,100m)

Novice
Start from the 300m and work down back up   1,200m

Intermediate
Stop after the 100 easy   1,600m

Advanced
                                                                3,100m

Total distance   **1,900–4,500m**

SWIM SESSION 16

Session objective: Technical endurance 3 of 4

Teaching point
Hand positioning and strength – these exercises will help you hold more water, making the water around the hand feel more solid. A solid hand position is necessary to allow the body to move forwards over the hand.

Fists/fingers splayed
Relaxed swimming with fins. Swim alternate lengths, fists clenched/fingers wide apart. Make use of the forearm while the hand size is diminished. Add a central snorkel to allow full concentration on the hands.
   Rest 30

Single fists/fingers splayed
Relaxed swimming with alternate lengths, as follows:
Right hand fist clenched, left hand normal
Left hand fist clenched, right hand normal
Into 50m normal hands and repeat the 100m sequence
Make use of the forearm while the hand size is diminished. Try to maintain similar levels of propulsion despite the discrepancies in hand shape/size
   Rest 30

SPS (single paddle swimming)
Relaxed swimming with a single paddle swum as:
50m right hand normal, left hand with the paddle
50m left hand normal, right hand with a paddle
50m both paddles and repeat the sequence
Try to maintain similar levels of propulsion despite the discrepancies in hand shape/size
   Rest 30

Fists/fingers played
Relaxed swimming, but this time with a pull buoy. Swim alternate lengths, fists clenched/fingers wide apart. Make use of the forearm while the hand size is diminished. Made a little harder without the legs to assist. Utilize the foream to compensate. Pivot early at the elbow.
   Rest 30

Novice
Swim each drill as a 150m swim (600m)

SWIM SESSION 16 (*continued*)

Intermediate
Swim each drill as a 300m swim (1,200m)

Advanced
Swim each drill as a 400m swim (1,600m)

Hand strength routine
(300–1,200m)
(3–12) × 100m FC in the following manner, rest 20 between 100m; feel the hands getting bigger as you progress until you almost feel as if you have invisible paddles on for the full stroke:

25m *fists*: Try to minimize the hands slipping through the water by keeping the forearm vertical
25m *pointing*: Point the index finger down to the bottom of the pool, firm at the wrist, bent at the elbow
25m OK position with the index finger and thumb lightly touching
25m *fingers* open (wide apart for a half length), then just a subtle change at halfway to close the hands slightly

Total distance   **1,200–2,800m**

SWIM SESSION 17

Session objective: Technical endurance 4 of 4

Teaching point
Consider the arm movements in these drills a distraction to the leg kick. We will start out with the legs as the main focus and then add more complex arm movements during the drills sequence. Slowly we rebuild towards full stroke FC, and hopefully maintain a good continuous kick. So often the kick is interrupted with a large splayed position or without a continuous rhythm.

Streamlined kick
Position the body with the upper inside arms pressed tightly against the ears. Arms outstretched, hands furthest away from the top of the head. Palms down, one on top of the other. Legs only kicking from the hips. Attempt a small continuous movement, big toes brushing against each other to a fast rhythm. Aim for loose ankles, soft knees, and legs predominantly straight originating from the hip not the knee. Works best with a central snorkel; if not, lift the head to breathe.

Alternate a length of kick with fins, then into full stroke on the even lengths. If a full length of kick is beyond you, then swim a half-length and complete the length full stroke FC.

Rest 20sec between lengths

Progress towards less fin use

Brams kick
Breaststroke arms with FC legs. We start with a simple arm movement so can still fully focus on the legs. In this position the arms should not be too much of a distraction. Keep in mind all the FC kick pointers from the previous kick drill.

Alternate 2 lengths of Brams kick with fins with 2 lengths of full stroke on the even swims. If a full length of kick is beyond you, then swim a half-length and complete the length full stroke FC.

Rest 20sec between 50m swims

Extension position
Rather than focus on streamline, we use this position to focus on kicking while on your side, which is a little more challenging than when you are flat. Maintain the big toes tapping while turning to breathe. The temptation will be to splay the legs to counterbalance the head turn.

Swim single lengths, rest 10 between each, odd swims with the left arm leading, even swims with the right arm leading. Fins for all but the very advanced. Can't use fins? Try half a length, then finish the length full stroke.

SWIM SESSION 17 (continued)

10-kick catch-up
10-kick catch-up is swum with 10 kicks while in the caught-up position (streamlined with both arms out in front): on the tenth kick either the left or right then completes a single arm cycle. Once complete, another 10 kicks are performed, then the opposite arm cycles through. The arm movements now become a little more technical, but you are being challenged to maintain all the previous kick pointers.

Swim as 50m, rest 20 between each, 2 with fins, 2 without

Catch-up drill
Full catch-up – hands meet while outstretched in front. Leading hand out in front, until the other hand catches up and touches, and go. Now there is no pause between the arm cycles, causing you perhaps not to be fully focused on the leg kick. Resist this temptation, reread the kick pointers from the first drill above, and refocus on the legs. Odd lengths catch-up, even lengths full stroke.

Novice
Swim each block as a 150m swim (750m)

Intermediate
Swim each block as a 300m swims (1,500m)

Advanced
Swim each block as a 400m swim (2,000m)

Bringing it all together
Swim 1L of each of these to make a varied 100m combining all the drills. Start out with a simple arm movement so as to focus on the legs 100 per cent. Slowly rebuild towards the full stroke, hoping to keep that small flutter kick from the hip bubbling under the surface; big toes brushing against each other.

4–12 sets of the following 100m swim:
1L breaststroke arms with FC legs Brams kick
1L 10-kick catch-up
1L full catch-up
1L full stroke
Attempt the first two 100m with fins, and then 3 and 4 without

Total distance: 1,150–3,200m

SWIM SESSION 18

Session objective: Swim test 1 of 4

Teaching point

Swim golf is a great way of learning an optimum stroke rate. At one level this is a great intro 'test swim' on its own, but as you progress you need to be challenged further, so we then attempt 'a round of.'

Basic golf

Simply add the time taken to complete 25m, and add the number of strokes taken. Aim to keep the numbers similar – so 22 strokes and 22sec = a score of 44.

If you speed up yet lose good technique, then the overall score remains high, as stroke count usually increases. Similarly if you glide and kick too much to lower your stroke count, the overall score stays high as time increases. Keep an eye on your golf score mid-session, during fitness sessions, and so on.

You do not need a ridiculously low score to swim well. In fact we usually use this as an alarm bell warning to let us know if technique is deteriorating during a main set. Watch out for scores going up mid-session.

Novice

Aim to swim under 25 strokes per 25m – 1 stroke per 1m

Intermediate

Aim to break a golf score of 50 – 25 strokes and 25sec

Advanced

Can contemplate 'a round of golf', as follows:

Round of golf

Once you have an average golf score you can use this as a measure and to check for improvements. You have x seconds to swim 25m and then take a 'recovery'. The balance between the time it took to swim the length and the chosen rest period is your rest. A fairly challenging option could be as follows, but start sensibly with an interval where you get 15sec rest at least.

Round 1

12 × 25m off 40sec – you have 40sec to swim 1 length. If you achieve it in 25sec you then take 15sec 'recovery'.

SWIM SESSION 18 (*continued*)

In addition we could aim for 25sec and 22 strokes over 25m – a golf score of 47 or under on each length, and look to maintain this score. With this much rest hopefully you will be able to maintain your average throughout.

Take a well-earned 100m easy recovery swim before continuing with Round 2.

Round 2

8 × 25m off 35sec – you now have 35sec to swim 1 length, and if completed in 25sec you then take 10sec rest.

An aim could be for 25sec and 22 strokes over 25m – a golf score of 47 or under on each length, with less rest. This will be harder to maintain now with less rest. You might see the score increase, as fitness and technique need to catch up. Maybe revisit this 'interval' in a month and see if you complete all eight at your designated golf score.

100m easy recovery.

Round 3

4 × 25m off 30sec – you have 30sec to swim 1 length in 25sec, then take 5sec rest. To finish it would be hard, but the aim would be for 25sec and 22 strokes over 25m – a golf score of 47 or under on each length with very little rest.

Swim golf

Aim to maintain 'par' throughout as the rest period decreases.

SWIM SESSION 19

Session objective: Swim test 2 of 4

Teaching point
An 'add-up' main set will give the confidence that a fast standard swim is possible! It will also predict a likely race-day swim time. The many wall push-offs will be negated by the wetsuit effect in open water.

Main set
Novice
Start a watch as the first 50m commences
30 × 50m, rest 15. Stop the watch as the last 50m finishes
Subtract the total rest block of 7:15
This means start at 0, finish at 32:15 having swum 30 times 50m, resting 15 between each 50m. This gives a 1,500m time of 25:00

Intermediate
20 × 100m, rest 15 between each 100m
Record the first 5 × 100m, then record numbers 7, 9, 11, 13, 15 before recording the last 5 for an add-up 1,500m again. The even swims in the middle are not to be a swim-down, but do take the pressure off the pace slightly

Advanced
Swim the odd 100m controlled and relaxed, but not as a swim-down
30 × 100m, rest 10 after the odd swims, 15 after the even swims Record all even swims individually for an add-up 1,500m – e.g. average 1:29s and you could call that a 22:15 approx swim

Total distance: **1,500–3,000m**

SWIM SESSION 20

Session objective: Swim test 3 of 4

Teaching point

A three-part straight swim. A test to be performed each training cycle to measure and gauge improvements. A continuous test set – swim as far as you can in 20min within the following guidelines:

4min of FC kick with a 'pull-kick' float that can then be used for the next pull swim
6min of FC pull – keep the leg kick to a minimum. Dump the float at the 10min mark
10min of FC swim – use a watch to mark out the time changes if you do not have a colleague/coach to blow a whistle

Count the number of lengths swum for a total metres score: this should be recorded and used to gauge improvements. The nature of this swim somewhat mimics that of an open-water event. Strong legs help with a fast start, the easier mid-section and the final strong finish where the legs are reintroduced to start the vascular shunt process of getting blood to the legs for the bike.

The ability to start fast in swimming is essential; this can be practised over and over again during training sessions.

SWIM SESSION 21

Session objective: Swim test 4 of 4

Teaching point
A broken main set that needs to be recorded will be a time to evaluate how the technique is holding up under a little pressure. This set does not offer enough rest to recover fully, but just enough to keep speed up. It will provide a reasonably accurate predictor of a likely race time.

Novice: standard distance
(1,500m)
Start a watch to record the set's overall duration.
3 × 200m strong steady pace, rest 30 (including 30sec after the third 200m)
Progress straight into:
5 × 100m strong steady pace, rest 20 (including 20sec after the fifth 100m)
Progress straight into:
8 × 50m strong steady pace, rest 10 (including 10sec after the eighth 50m)
(Stop your overall time at the conclusion of the second 50m swim)
Subtract 4min 20sec from this time for your broken 1,500m time.

Intermediate: Half Ironman®
(1,900m)
Start a watch to record the set's overall duration.
3 × 300m strong steady pace, rest 30 (including 30sec after the third 300m)
Progress straight into:
3 × 200m strong steady pace, rest 20 (including 20sec after the third 200m)
Progress straight into:
3 × 100m strong steady pace, rest 10 (including 10sec after the third 100m)
Progress straight into:
2 × 50m strong steady pace, rest 5 (stop your overall time at the conclusion of the second 50m swim)
Subtract 3min 05sec from this time for your broken 1,900m time.

Advanced: Ironman®
(3,800m)
Start a watch to record the set's overall duration.
4 × 400m strong steady pace, rest 30 (including 30sec after the fourth 400m)
Progress straight into:
4 × 300m strong steady pace, rest 20 (including 20sec after the fourth 300m)

SWIM SESSION 21 (continued)

Progress straight into:
4 × 200m strong steady pace, rest 10 (including 10sec after the fourth 200m)
Progress straight into:
4 × 50m strong steady pace, rest 5 (stop your overall time at the conclusion of the fourth 50m swim)
Subtract 4min 15sec from this time for your broken 3,800m time.

Total distance   **1,500–3,800m**

SWIM SESSION 22

Session objective: Pool-based open-water (OW) skills, 1 of 3

Teaching point
Each part of the main set has an open-water theme that will bring something to your skill set on race day, enabling you to overcome many of the scenarios that might arise. Ideally you will need some teammates for these to work.

Main set
Tunnel of fun
With as many people as you have, line up in two columns, side by side and facing each other, 1m apart from your side-on neighbour and 1.5m apart from your opposite neighbour, forming a tunnel. One end is designated the start, the other is the end. Each swimmer swims through the tunnel while 'teammates' splash and make waves. The swimmer then joins the column and the next swimmer starts.
(This works well in the pool with one column of splashers facing the pool wall. Now the swimmer gets a chance to breathe away from the splash.)

Vascular shunt and derivatives
Depending on the swim environment, this could be as simple as a hard 200m swum in a 25m pool with an exit and immediate re-entry at both ends, which will really elevate the HR. If space and the swim environment allows, aim for a hard 100m swim, exit, loosen velcro and zip, followed by a 100m run back to the re-entry point and repeat. The idea

SWIM SESSION 22 (*continued*)

is to get used to blood flow in the upper body quickly flowing to the lower limbs for a controlled run to TI.

Circle swims
A couple of options here: both styles will promote sighting, competitiveness, and an arcing style of FC around a large buoy.

At least ten swimmers create a large circle in the pool or open-water shallows, of 30m circumference if possible:

As a 'duel': Two swimmers could start at opposites and swim until one is caught. Could take a while!

As a single circle relay: One half of the circle are team A, the other B. Two swimmers start at opposite sides and swim a full lap before returning to their spot. Their teammate is the person on their left, whom they tag. The relay continues. Ensure even numbers.

Multiple circles could race against each other if numbers allow. One circle is one team, and a full lap of all swimmers completes.

Open-water relays
(Square and triangle) speed and sighting are essential to win this!
A team of four (triangle) or five (square) challenge each other. The course is set up with three members A, B, C making a large equilateral triangle. A and D stand together. Swimmer A sprints to B, B to C, C to D and D continues on to A. The relay is complete once members are back to where they started. As a square, A sprints to B, B to C, C to D, D to E, E to A and so on.

Slalom
Fast turns and quick sighting are essential here to get down the slalom fast.
Two columns are created with your side-on neighbour 4m apart. Your opposite neighbour is 45 degrees offset and again 4m away. The challenge is to swim down the course keeping the left column of buoys on your left and the right column on your right as you sprint between them, sighting and making fast turns.

Total distance   **Group-dependent**

SWIM SESSION 23

Session objective: Pool-based OW skills, 2 of 3

Teaching point
If you can experience some of the less pleasant aspects of OW in training, they will not faz you on race day.

Breathing pattern practice
FC swum as 1L breathing to the left, 1L breathing to the right, third length breathing bilaterally, every third.
  Rest 45
  On race day you will probably feel more comfortable breathing every second stroke. If you could choose the side you breathe to as conditions dictate then you would be at a great advantage over your competitors. Those who have not practised will be obliged to breathe into the flailing arm of a competitor or looking straight into the sun.

Breath-holding
FC swum as no breathers once the lane rope turns to red at both ends (on the way into the wall and on the way out – that is, 5–7sec of breath-holding at the end of each length). This may not have happened yet, but it might, and it would be good not to be panicked when it does. During periods of congestion at the start or around a turn you may not be in a position to get a breath in when it suits. A few seconds of breath-holding will help you ride this time out.
  Rest 45

No-rest swim
FC swum continuously, no touching the wall. As soon as your lane ropes change to red, then loop through in front of the wall to simulate a long continuous swim with no hanging on and resting. If the lane is wide enough and you have pool space, then you might want to practise the backstroke roll to speed up your turn.
  Rest 45

Sighting
FC swum as seven strokes powerful FC, then relax into two easy, and pop up to sight forwards. Just the eyes above the surface though, don't waste time or energy lifting the whole head up and simultaneously breathing. You should practise getting your breath in during your normal strokes, and using the sighting strokes to sight.
  Rest 45

Relaxing and goggle emptying

FC swum as seven strokes FC, then roll into an exaggerated extension position facing up, lead arm outstretched. Use this time to catch your breath, take advantage of the buoyancy of the wetsuit, and relax for a moment: empty your goggles if need be, and steady your nerves after any minor altercation in the swim!

Rest 45

Novice:

Swim each block as 150m swims

Intermediate

Swim each block as 300m swims

Advanced

Swim each block as 500m swims

Total distance   **1,500–2,500m**

Attempt to keep the lower goggle submerged when breathing.

SWIM SESSION 24

Session objective: Pool-based OW skills, 3 of 3

Teaching point
Some teammates will make this session more effective; you will be surrounded by swimmers on race day, so start now. Get familiar with swimming in small groups, side by side, elbow to elbow, and race day will not feel quite so claustrophobic.

Chain-gang
Works best with a group of five to six in the lane. Aside from the last person, the gang pushes off and swims slow on each other's feet to one side of the lane. The chain-gang needs to be tight and slow, to allow the last swimmer a fighting chance of sprinting the length and getting to the other end before the 'gang'. The 'sprinter' then leads the chain-gang and recovers, which will help keep the 'gang' from speeding up too much. The new last person now sprints to the front for lap 2. Continue looping though until all have sprinted two to three times, or the time/distance expires.
   Rest 45

Vascular shunt exits
FC swum strongly. As you approach each deep end wall you climb out, stand up, and return to the water. Not a full vascular shunt exercise, but it does make a standard swim a lot harder.
   Rest 45

Three abreast
FC swum continuously three abreast in a lane for 1L hard. When the final group of three finish in your lane, the lead group of three can continue. Not really drafting practice here, more just getting used to the jostle of shoulder-to-shoulder swimming.
   Rest 45

Blind swim
FC swum on top of the black line. Last person to finish 25m before the leader pushes off for repeat 2 is the rest period. Alternate three strokes eyes open with five closed. Keep the hand pathways central, the breathing bilateral, and the backbone on top of the black line, and once the eyes reopen you should still find yourself on top of the black line, having swum straight.
   Rest 45

SWIM SESSION 24 (*continued*)

Snakes and ladders

Start the group in one corner; each swimmer swims 2L in each lane starting on the left of the lane (anti-clockwise) if entering the left side of the pool. Duck under the lane ropes for lengths 3 and 4. A full pool swim could be from 200m to 400m depending on the number of lanes and the length of the pool. The faster swimmers can exit, return to the entry point and start again until either the last swimmer is caught or the last swimmer finishes the full course.

   Rest 45

Novice

Swim each block as 150m swims

Intermediate

Swim each block as 300m swims

Advanced

Swim each block as 500m swims

Total distance   **750–2,500m**

SWIM SESSION 25

Session objective: Open-water fitness, 1 of 3

Always swim in a safe open-water environment with at least one partner, with proper supervision, and with safety cover.

Teaching point

A time-based style of fitness block of work fondly known as the 'pyramid of pain' due to the increase in the middle. Would work ideally in a small body of water. Create a small marked-out square or triangle with marker buoys. Single whistle blown at the end of a hard swim stops swimmers; double blow indicates resume to faster swimming.

First swim: 1min hard swim, and then rest 1min easy swimming or treading water
Second swim: 2min hard swim, 1min easy swimming
Third swim: 3min hard swim, 1min easy swimming
Fourth swim: 4min hard swim, 1min easy swimming
Fifth swim: 5min hard swim, 1min easy swimming
Optional: 6min swim, 1min easy swimming
5min hard swim, 1min easy swimming
4min hard swim, 1min easy swimming
3min hard swim, 1min easy swimming
2min hard swim, 1min easy swimming
1min hard swim, 1min easy swimming
(47min)

If limited for time, then a 1, 2, 3, 4, 3, 2, 1 generates a 29min main set.

Total distance   Swimmer dependent

In an open-water swim, the ability to sight and to draft is a must!

SWIM SESSION 26

Session objective: Open-water fitness, 2 of 3

Teaching point

If you are fortunate enough to have a body of water available where you can safely and quickly enter/exit repeatedly, then there are many fitness options available.

One of my favourite venues for working on the Vascular Shunt principle is Hyde Park Lido; with the short jetty equipped with steps, you can haul yourself up, exit onto the edge of the water and run 100m before re-entering the water.

Exiting to T1 can be quite traumatic for the inexperienced triathlete, with the blood rushing to the legs to start the run to your bike. In order to help this key area the following OW routine will focus on helping you to get comfortable.

Novice

Aim for 2 × 7mins with 2mins recovery. The 7mins involves constant swimming (50–100m) into a short run if the location allows. Be steady on the exit, and jog steady on the run. Be careful with your footing.

Intermediate

Aim for 25min of swim/run practice. Add to the effect by releasing the Velcro on your suit and pulling the wetsuit zip up/down during the short run. Ideally you would have a coach/helper to rezip your suit and close the Velcro flap.

Advanced

Aim for 40min, which may take some building up towards. The fitness effect of swimming and then running, shunting blood from the shoulders to the legs, will be dramatic. Warm up the lower limbs ahead of time to prevent any cramping. The elevated HR from the run will leave you fatigued as you re-enter the water, and you need to really refocus on good technique to get back up to a good swimming pace.

SWIM SESSION 27

Session objective: Open-water fitness, 3 of 3

Teaching point
The ladder set. Here we are looking for consistent pacing in open water. You will need some kind of marked-out course so you can swim to distance and keep to a time. A 100m-sided square or triangle could work well

Novice
(900m)
100, 200, 300, 200, 100 at an even pace.
Rest 10sec after the 100m swims, 20 after the 200m swims, and 30 after the 300m swim.

Intermediate
(1,700m)
100, 200, 300, 200, 100, 200, 300, 200, 100 at an even pace.
Rest 10sec after the 100m swims, 20 after the 200m swims, 30 after the 300m swims.

Advanced
(3,600m)
Two sets of the following:

100, 200, 300, 200, 100, 100, 200, 300, 200, 100 at an even pace.
Rest 10sec after the 100m swims, 20 after the 200m swims, 30 after the 300m swims.

If you swim 2min for the 100m, then aim for 4min on the 200m and 6min on the 300m to obtain even pacing. Just a guideline, your 100m swim will dictate the other swims.

Total distance   **900–3,600m**

SWIM SESSION 28

Session objective: Race taper 1 of 3.

Teaching point

The key thing to keep in mind when tapering is that you are now just fine-tuning your approach. Not much can be added, so get your rest and allow yourself to arrive on the start line ready to go. Do not overdo it, as you could detract from the great work you have done in the months leading up to race day. If on a certain day your body does not like the session, then ease back. Taper time psychologically is a tough time, and sometimes the body just doesn't feel great. Work out a race pace time you had in mind, and divide that up into the distances and use these as an aim on the building distance sets. The example 'pacing' suggestions are just that, and you will find your own.

1) 50m FC, 100m FC, 150m FC, 200m FC, 250m FC at a constant pace. All with just 15sec rest. As an example, if you hit 45sec on the first 50m, constant pace suggests 3:45min on the 250m swim.
Continue straight into 4 × 50m FC, with 30sec rest as technically accurate as possible. Not a swim-down, but certainly relaxed ahead of the next build block.

2) 50m FC, 100m FC, 150m FC, 200m FC at a constant pace. All with just 15sec rest. If you hit 45sec on the first 50m, constant pace suggests 3min on the 200m swim.
Continue straight into 4 × 50m FC, with 20sec rest as technically accurate as possible.

3) 50m FC, 100m FC, 150m FC at a constant pace. All with just 15sec rest. If you hit 45sec on the first 50m, constant pace suggests 2:25 on the 150m.
Continue straight into 4 × 50m FC. With 10sec rest as technically accurate as possible.

4) 50m FC, 100m FC, all at a constant pace. All with just 15sec rest. If you hit 45sec on the first 50m constant pace suggests 90sec on the 100m.
Continue straight into 4 × 50m FC with 5sec rest as technically accurate as possible.

5) 50m FC at a strong race pace. With just 15sec rest.
Continue straight into 4 × 50m FC off 90sec, as technically accurate as possible

Novices perform nos 3–5: 1,100m
Intermediates perform nos 2–5: 2,000m
Advanced perform nos 1–5: 3,150m

SWIM SESSION 29

Session objective: Race taper 2 of 3

Teaching point
Maintain pacing. An excellent combination to gear you up to a constant race pace. As fatigue sets in after the middle swims on the main set due to so little rest, you will still have to work hard to meet the final swim aim and keep on pace. Start steady.

Novice
(750m)
5 × 150m swum as follows: rest 45 between each 150m swim.
(IL FC, 2L FC, 3L FC rest 10 between each swim.) 2L pace is double the time it took to do IL, 3L pace is triple the time it took to do the IL;
e.g., 40sec for IL, 1:20 for 2L so 2:00 is 3L.
Fatigue sets in after the 2L due to so little rest, but then you will still have to work hard to meet the 3L aim.

Intermediate
(1,800m)
6 × 300m swum as follows: rest 45 between each 300m swim
(2L FC, 4L FC, 6L FC, rest 10 between each swim.) 4L pace is double the time it took to do 2L, 6L pace is triple the time it took to do the 2L;
e.g., 1:10 for 2L, 2:20 for 4L so 3:30 is 6L.
Fatigue sets in after the 4L due to so little rest, but then you will still have to work hard to meet the 6L aim.

Advanced
(2,700m)
6 × 450m swum as follows: rest 45 between each 450m swim.
(3L FC, 6L FC, 9L FC rest 10.) 6L pace is double the time it took to do 3L, 9L pace is triple the time it took to do the 3L; e.g., 1:15 for 3L, 2:30 for 6L so 3:45 is 9L.
Fatigue sets in after the 6L due to so little rest, but then you will still have to work hard to meet the 9L aim.

Total distance: **750–2,700m**

SWIM SESSION 30

Session objective: Race taper 3 of 3

Teaching point
Set out at a slow, sensible pace: you will have a long way to go once committed to this main set. Distance swum increases, but rest does not, simulating race day fatigue. Start out conservatively with this one! The lack of rest hurts; you don't actually need to start to swim faster.

Main set
2L (50m) FC at 70 per cent effort, rest 10
4L (100m) FC at 70 per cent effort, rest 10
6L (150m) FC at 70 per cent effort, rest 10
8L (200m) FC at 70 per cent effort, rest 10

10L (250m) FC at 70 per cent effort, rest 10	750m
through to 20L (500m)	2,750m

The idea is that you set a benchmark time on the first 2L, repeat and keep it constant. You can work through as far as you comfortably like as a guideline.

Novice
750m (last repeat is 250m)

Intermediate
1,800m (last repeat is 400m)

Advanced
2,750m (stop at 500m)

You can also use this set to target a race pace. Thus for 70min Ironman® pace, you would target:
55sec swim for 2L, rest 10, which leads to:
1:50sec swim for 4L, rest 10
2:45 swim for 6L, rest 10, and so on…

Total distance: **750–2,750m**

PART II
CYCLING

CHAPTER 4

CYCLING TECHNIQUE AND EQUIPMENT

Cycling is the single discipline in triathlon where equipment can make a difference to performance. It is most important that the bike is set up properly so that technique can be productive rather than wasted. This does not mean that the bike needs to be expensive, rather that it is the correct size for the athlete and is mechanically sound. It is essential that the bike and rider complement each other perfectly, combining comfort and mechanical efficiency, good aerodynamics and flexibility of a changing riding position so the athlete can cope with all racing and training conditions.

In the first instance, take advice from a mechanic in a cycle shop, but by listening and learning the athlete should soon be able to adjust the bike to suit his height, leg length and riding position. Instructions for setting up the bike position can only be guidelines, and must allow for individual preferences, strengths and weaknesses. If changing the riding and set-up position for any reason, make those changes gradually, because attempting to make too big a change at any one time will cause soreness and injury.

Modern bikes have a great range of adjustment, and bike size (within reasonable parameters) is not critical. Easy adjustments can be made to the saddle height, saddle front and rear position, handlebar height, and the stem length to give handlebar forward and back positions.

Having a clean bike is important, not just for esoteric reasons but primarily so that any structural and mechanical faults are not hidden by dirt. The athlete should methodically check the frame, wheels and tyres, freewheel and chain, brakes, headset, handlebars and stem, gears, chainwheel and bottom bracket, and the pedals.

Cycling has to overcome three main forces: air resistance (as you cycle, the wind hits you and slows you down), friction (the tyres rolling on the road surface, so ensure that they are pumped up to the recommended level) and gravity (riding up hills), so it is essential that your bike is set up properly and that your riding position is perfect.

Setting up the Correct Riding Position

Cyclists go to great lengths to ensure that their riding position is absolutely correct for them as individuals. There are a number of general rules that apply to setting the correct position, but each individual will have their own specific position that applies to them and ensures that they will get maximum force, power and fluidity of movement during cycle training and racing. The points of contact between the cyclist and the bike are saddle and backside, pedals and feet, and handlebars and hands.

Saddle Height and Position

The height of the saddle is all-important and should be set first. Sit on the saddle and place the left crank at the bottom of the stroke in line with the seat tube. Place the heel of the foot (wear the cycling or training shoes that you will normally ride in) on to the pedal: the leg should be almost straight but not over-stretched. If you are wearing cycling shoes, don't forget to add on the thickness of the shoe plate that clips into the pedal. A general rule for bike frame size is to take two-thirds of the inside leg size – thus a rider with a 32in inside leg would need a 21in frame size.

Make sure that the saddle is level (parallel to the top tube). With the height set, check the forward and backward position of the saddle to ensure that you are not too stretched out nor too bunched up. Sit on the saddle with your cycling shoes on and clipped into the pedals. Place the pedals in a horizontal position, and check that your knee is directly above the ball of the foot while it is clipped into the pedal. If the knee is not above the foot, adjust the saddle forwards or backwards until it is. Your fingertips should be just level or behind the back edge of the handlebars.

It is possible to replace the handlebar stem with one of a different length if this is necessary for optimum riding position. If there is a big change in the forward and back position, it may be necessary to readjust the saddle height.

Handlebar Height

With the essential height and forward positions fixed, set the handlebars so that the bottom of the bars where they flatten out are parallel to the top tube, then set the brake levers, ensuring they are facing directly forwards, and not tilting either too much up or down.

The height of the top of the handlebars should be between roughly level and 2in below the top of the saddle when you begin riding, but will gradually drop down as you become more confident. However, the handlebar height will depend on the flexibility of the rider. You must be comfortable with your hands on the drop position (bottom of the handlebars) and on the top of the handlebars, and it must be easy for you to reach the brakes.

Technique

As with swimming and running, a good cycle technique is essential to get the most from training.

Pedalling and Pedalling Drills

Pedalling is a circular action, but new cyclists and triathletes will instinctively pedal in a 'piston-type' up-and-down action. However, it is essential to train so that you start pedalling in the smoother circular action. A more equal load on different muscle groups is used in circular pedalling, and this will spread fatigue and push it back. This is crucial for triathletes who must run after the bike section. However, circular pedalling does not mean that equal pressure will be applied throughout the entire pedalling movement. It is important to maintain or increase the power on the piston up-and-down movement while at the same time improving circular movement cycling efficiency.

Try to relax when riding, and don't push 'big' gears. You should be trying to achieve 90 to 100 revolutions per min (rpm). If your pedal revolutions per min are fewer than 80, you are probably in too big a gear. Similarly, if you are pedalling at more than 100 revolutions per min, your gearing is probably too easy. Pushing big gears fatigues you quickly and makes it difficult to run well. However, having said this, there are some triathletes who can run well after pushing big gears – so guidelines are merely guidelines.

To increase power and efficiency, push the pedals across the top of the pedal stroke circle: this will create a longer power stroke by starting the application of force before the down-stroke begins – and keep that force on the pedal throughout.

We can use the analogy of the clock face to determine how and where pedal force should be applied to the pedal; we should also pedal in a direction that is 90 degrees to the crank arm. At the top of the pedal stroke (12 o'clock on our clock-face analogy) you should be moving the pedal forwards. At 6 o'clock push the pedal backwards. At exactly 3 o'clock you are pushing directly down, while at 2 or 4 o'clock you would be moving the pedal slightly forwards and down, or slightly back and down respectively. Push turns into pull through the bottom of the pedal stroke: this maintains a constant force through the entire pedalling circle, and balances the opposite leg pushing at the top of the pedal stroke.

A slight lift of the foot off the pedal as the pedal comes up at the rear also helps to balance and save energy. With the foot resting on the pedal, more resistance is created for the leg that is pushing down on the other pedal. Pulling up with great force is not necessary, just lifting slightly will balance the effort. Lift your knee as if you were walking up steep stairs or stepping on to a box.

Don't attempt everything at the same time. Focus on one aspect of efficient pedalling before moving on to the next. Put 'the full stroke' together in between the drills.

When practising drills for cycling, it is recommended that you use a turbo trainer (sometimes called the 'wind trainer'). Many of the training sessions in the next chapter rely heavily on the use of the turbo trainer. It means that total focus and concentration can be given to the session without having to worry about road conditions and dangerous traffic. Cycling on the road always has inherent danger, and when practising new drills, attention is focused on the drill.

The Power Phase

To increase the length of the power phase, imagine that you have stepped on some chewing gum and that it is now stuck to the bottom of your cycling shoe. As you approach the 5 o'clock position, rotate the ankle as if you were scraping the shoe, and maintain this scrape and rotation to the 7 o'clock position.

As your foot comes up the pull phase towards 11 o'clock, imagine kicking forwards hard with the toes up: push and kick your foot over the top as if trying to begin the push phase a little earlier, as this will increase the length of the power phase by beginning the power push earlier.

The least efficient phases of pedalling are the ones at the top and bottom of the circle, between 6 and 7 o'clock and between 12 and 2 o'clock. If you concentrate on your legs moving and changing throughout the entire circle you will maintain power better; this will combine the earlier drills and overcome the dead spots.

Drill: Single Leg Pedalling

Pedalling with one leg will emphasize and exaggerate the faults in the pedal action. Pedalling with both legs will cover up any weak or dead spots as the leg in the 'push' position will compensate for the leg pulling.

Rest one leg on a chair placed next to the turbo trainer, select an easy gear and start pedalling with one leg. You will be aware very quickly if you have chosen too big a gear as your upper leg muscles will fatigue very quickly. Pedal right-legged for one min, then switch to the left leg; repeat five times.

It takes a lot of effort to pull through the

bottom of the pedal stroke and lift the pedal back up and over the top. Focus on eliminating the dead spots at the bottom and top of the pedalling circle, and keep the pedalling motion as even and smooth as possible. This will be difficult at first, but improvements are quick on this drill. Don't use too small a gear, as easy momentum will circle the pedal up over the top.

Keep the legs relaxed and smooth. If there is any change in the sound and noise of the tyre on the rollers, it is probable that there is not a constant and efficient circling motion.

Drill: Developing Cadence and Leg Speed

Most cyclists ride at between 85 and 105 revolutions per minute (rpm), but individuals are different and you may be at the top or bottom of the range. This drill will help you develop cadence, but you should also test yourself on a measured course in different gears, and see how cadence affects your speed.

For this drill select an easy gear and start pedalling, gradually increasing cadence (speed of pedalling) until it is difficult to keep still on the saddle – you will feel as if you're bouncing up and down on the saddle. Gradually bring the cadence down until you've stopped bouncing, and maintain that cadence for between 15 to 30sec. Slow down the cadence until you recover, and then repeat the drill. Try to keep the pedalling action smooth and relaxed throughout. As with the single leg drill, any change in the sound and noise of the tyre on the rollers means an inefficient pedalling action.

As with all drills, concentrate on doing them properly at a slow speed to begin, then increase the speed. With cycling it is important that you attempt these drills in the position on the bike that you will be racing in, your racing position. This will normally mean with your hands at the bottom of the handlebars.

Strength Work

There is a need for strength and power as fitness progresses on the bike discipline. There is still a need to emphasize the circular pedalling action, even though the cadence will necessarily be slower.

Select a big, challenging gear that you can pedal at 60 to 70 rpm; stay in this gear for 1min, then select an easy gear and pedal at 100 rpm plus for 2min. Repeat five to six times.

Gearing and Cadence

Most evidence points to the benefits of high rpm/cadence throughout the cycle section, and particularly at its end, and it is crucial to select the appropriate gearing to maintain this. Play around with gearing and cadence. Don't assume that because a particular cadence feels 'right' just now, that it is right. Increasing cadence in training will make it feel right in racing.

If you have no experience of working at high rpm, start as appropriate and work for just one min at 100 rpm, gradually work up time, and also work up to and over 100 rpm – we've used 130 rpm at times. The following drill should help you in this.

One-legged Drill

(Use a chair to support the resting foot and leg.)

Focus on the two 'dead' spots, at the top of the stroke and at the bottom

Push the knee through and forwards

Drop the toes and 'scrape off' the foot

Start with an easy gear so there is little pressure, and work up to bigger gearing – as a rule of thumb, around 60/70rpm to begin with

Start with 30sec of single leg, 30sec both legs

Then to 60sec single leg, 60sec both legs

Then to 60sec right leg, 60sec left leg, and repeat

Big gears require a slow cadence (sitting) – beware knee damage – again with the focus on the two dead spots.

Dealing with Resistance

The things that hold us back from cycling faster are gravity, rolling resistance and wind resistance, and good aerodynamic form is important to overcome at least two of these. However, once aerodynamic form is perfect, we have to look at further ways to increase speed. The obvious one is fitness, but even before this applies, comes the correct choice and use of gears and cadence. The secret of fast cycling is finding the perfect trade-off between the size of the gear that you use and the speed of pedal revolutions, and the two classic mistakes at either end of the spectrum are:

- Selecting too big a gear and being forced to pedal so slowly against the high resistance that fatigue is almost immediate
- 'Overspinning' – selecting so small a gear that however high your cadence you are going to make little progress.

Choosing the correct gearing is crucial, although it is worth noting that there is no single correct cadence for everyone, bearing in mind individual cadence, speed, heart rate, perceived effort, fatigue and the ability to run off the bike. The following are important points to consider:

- The use of high gears tends to be a strength exercise
- The recovery rate on low gears is faster than on high gears
- The constant use of high gears in time trials may restrict the ability to compete successfully in triathlon
- The use of low gears from a young age tends to develop suppleness and flexibility in a rider

- In time trials, fast rides have been done by some riders using high gears, and these riders have developed an appropriate technique for this purpose. However, we are triathletes, not pure cyclists, and we have to consider the run afterwards as well
- When in doubt, it is always better to undergear to start with

Research on economical cadence (particularly Hagberg '81) has tended to demonstrate a most economical efficiency of between 90 and 100 revolutions per min. However, it is essential to remember that each triathlete is an individual, and just because 90 to 100rpm is the norm or median, it doesn't necessarily have to be appropriate for everybody. To re-emphasize, triathletes must be able to run when they get off the bike.

A rule of thumb which may help the individual to determine their best cadence is this: if the heart is pounding the revs are too high; if the leg muscles are crying out for relief the gear is too big and the revs too low. The chart opposite may help to indicate the range of gears to choose in particular racing and training circumstances. Please note that the heart rates set out are for demonstration only, and individual heart rate will vary with age, fitness and generic traits. There are many 'cycling clinics' where the heart rate can be measured and the relevant parameters set out for you.

Bike Handling Skills and Drills

Smooth Gear Changing

The secret to smooth gear changing is to plan ahead. Be ready for hills and change into an easier gear earlier than you think you will need to; this is particularly important for hills, as you will lose momentum as soon as you start climbing. You must keep pedalling as you change gear and maintain pressure on the pedals.

Maintaining Speed through Turns and Corners
Keep up your momentum through turns. Applying the brakes when there is no need means that you have to use a lot of energy to get back up to speed after the turn. New riders are usually very cautious and will do this often. Change down a gear before the turn, stop pedalling, and lean the bike into the corner. Again, new riders are cautious of leaning the bike, though be assured there is little danger here. But cornering and turning do

take away speed, and standing as you come out of the turn and pedalling hard will regain the speed more quickly. However, a lot of energy is used when standing on the pedals, so be cautious about this.

Controlling Speed
If you find you are going too fast in a turn, you must lean into the curve. It is better to increase your cornering angle. Put your weight on the outside (of the turn) pedal, as this will give the tyres more grip. Brake early rather than late. Putting on the brakes at the end of a turn will tend to straighten out the bike, which

Heart Rate Parameters

Intensity	Heart rate range	Purpose
level 1	below 135 bpm	Short rides for recovery Very long aerobic-type fat-burning sessions
tempo (tempo sessions take in a largish range of HRs)		
tempo	135–165 bpm	Development of economy and efficiency with high-volume work. The wide zone is useful for long sessions but the majority of time should be spent below 155bpm
level 2	155–165 bpm	Development of aerobic capacity with moderate-volume work at a controlled intensity. This should normally be done alone or with a small group. It can be done on the turbo, but there is the element of possible boredom here
level 3	170–180 bpm	Raising anaerobic threshold and acclimatization to race speed. This can be done • on a turbo • for controlled periods within a shortened tempo session • in a 10-mile or 25-mile time trial
level 4	180 bpm plus	High-intensity interval training to increase maximum power and improve lactate tolerance. It is most conveniently and safely done on a turbo trainer. Level four sessions should only be done when rested and recovered. Heart rates are not necessarily the best accurate guide for this type of intensity work. The training should rely more on perceived effort, with the HR being used and monitored for feedback

is the opposite of what you need it to do. Light braking on the rear wheel can help, but if it catches and seizes, release it immediately. Do not use your front brake in a turn, as the front wheel will slide away.

Sighting, Steering, Direction and Control
Don't only look directly in front of your front wheel, but look further ahead and check the whole corner before you enter it. Be aware of the best riding line all the way through the corner, and follow it: your bike will go where you look. Even for riding in a straight line, focus ahead and don't look down at the front wheel: looking too close means correcting line and control and is unsafe.

Training with a Group

Riding in a group quickly instils confidence, and group riding on the long endurance rides that are necessary as a part of training is recommended. To begin with, ride at a relatively slow speed with a smooth pedal action, one rider behind the other with a gap of one to two feet. Riders should aim for similar cadence by choosing a similar gear. To avoid freewheeling, this drill can be performed on a gentle hill slope. Riders will learn to be confident by following, and if anything does go wrong, it is easy just to put a foot down on the ground. As confidence increases, two lines can be formed instead of one, so the rider has someone beside as well as in front of and behind them. Gradually close the gap between yourself and the rider in front of you.

Riders should take turns in front of the line,

and the change should be made in the following way: the lead rider should check over their shoulder for any danger, then move to one side and slow the cadence slightly. The next rider takes the lead not by accelerating but by maintaining speed, as the previous lead rider gradually drops back down the line; he/she should stay close as they pass the other riders while doing this. As he/she drops towards the back of the line, they should accelerate slightly as their front wheel draws level with the back rider's rear wheel. This will give the slight impetus needed to move in immediately without letting a gap open.

Group riding on long endurance rides is a necessary part of training.

CHAPTER 5

THE CYCLE SESSIONS

The thirty cycle sessions can be attempted on the road or on the turbo trainer. For the more specific interval sessions – and also some of the hill sessions – I recommend the turbo, as any adverse road conditions will not come into play and the rider can be totally focused on the biking effort. The sessions cover endurance, interval training, hill repetitions, speed and power, and technique. There is also a strong focus on using target heart rates on many sessions. The specific interval (including hill repetition) sessions are particularly recommended. There are many triathletes who survive by only long, easy cycle sessions, and are then surprised when it starts to hurt during the bike discipline of the race when speed is applied!

Cycle session 1: Self-testing, increasing demand, assessing fitness
Cycle session 2: 'Classic' anaerobic threshold session
Cycle session 3: Lactate tolerance
Cycle session 4: Anaerobic threshold
Cycle session 5: Progressive resistance and increasing demand
Cycle session 6: Speed endurance/increasing demand
Cycle session 7: Anaerobic threshold, increasing demand, cadence
Cycle session 8: Smoothness and cadence
Cycle session 9: Fast cadence and the use of big gears
Cycle session 10: Increasing demand with endurance

Cycle session 11: Increasing demand with endurance
Cycle session 12: Hill climbing
Cycle session 13: Extended speed and power
Cycle session 14: Pushing big gears while maintaining cadence
Cycle session 15: Climbing long, sapping hills
Cycle session 16: Progressive, increasing demand
Cycle session 17: Maintaining speed and cadence under pressure
Cycle session 18: Maintaining race speed after initial fast start
Cycle session 19: Changing gears, maintaining speed under pressure
Cycle session 20: Pushing the anaerobic threshold
Cycle session 21: Pushing the anaerobic threshold
Cycle session 22: Improving race speed under pressure
Cycle session 23: Sustaining power and speed
Cycle session 24: Sustaining race speed under continuous pressure
Cycle session 25: Maintaining speed when fatigued
Cycle session 26: Ironman® and half Ironman® simulation
Cycle session 27: Sustaining speed when tired
Cycle session 28: Working on strength when tired after speed
Cycle session 29: Power and sprint speed
Cycle session 30: Extended power and sprint speed

CYCLE SESSION 1

Session objective: Self-testing procedure, increasing demand, assessment of fitness

- It is essential to use a turbo trainer for this session. It is also very helpful to have a friend or coach to monitor this test with you.

Aim: To find your maximum HR, to find your level of fitness, and to check your level of fitness by re-testing.

When to use: All year, but not immediately before an important race.

Description
- Warm up for 10 to 15min until the heart rate (HR) is constant.
- Go into the big ring and bottom (easiest) gear (eg 52 × 22), and pedal at 95 rpm for 2min. Note your HR at the beginning and end of the 2min.
- Progress up through the gears every 2min, maintaining 95 rpm.
Note your HR at the beginning and end of every 2min.
- As the session becomes increasingly tiring, eventually the HR will level out, having risen constantly (although not necessarily consistently) throughout the test.
- This is probably not your maximum HR, so carry on pedalling by getting out of the saddle, until you reach exhaustion (this is where you need that friend or coach).
- Note your maximum HR as accurately as possible.
- Warm down (spin) in an easy gear, and note your HR recovery.

Variations
- If you are only just starting triathlon, or if you are very unfit, progress by 1min each time rather than 2min.
- If you are very experienced and/or very fit, progress by 4min each time rather than 2min.

CYCLE SESSION 2

Session objective: Extend 'classic' anaerobic threshold

The exercise physiologists tell us that a 6min effort at race pace, repeated between four to eight times at racing speed with minimal recovery, will fulfil the needs of adaptation for racing speed. For triathletes training on three disciplines, this fits in nicely with our programmes (overall on each discipline):

For swimming, 6 × 400m swim, and rest 6min (or 6.30/7.00 etc)
For cycling, 6 × 6min on the turbo, recovery 1min, spin
For running, 6 × 1 mile (or 1,500m, 1,200m etc), recovery 1min

Aim: To extend anaerobic threshold, deal with race pace fatigue.

When to use: All year.

Description
- Warm up for 10 to 15min. I prefer to do this session on a turbo trainer, as everything can be monitored rather than the biker needing to be aware of road conditions.
- 6 × 6min at just faster than 25 mile/40km racing pace.
- Recovery 1min in between.

Variations
You don't necessarily need to start your training programme with 6 × 6min! This is a far more demanding session than it appears on paper. You are aiming at faster than current race pace, and it needs concentration to maintain the speed and pressure throughout. You may need to begin at 4 × 4min with 90sec recovery, and gradually progress through 5 × 4min, 4 × 5, 5 × 5, 6 × 5, 5 × 6 and finally 6 × 6min.

CYCLE SESSION 3

Session objective: To learn about lactate tolerance

For age groupers the cycle discipline is largely a time trial, and this session replicates that with the appropriate heart rate: a 40min time trial in race position.

- This session, like many, is best done on the turbo trainer.

Aim: To understand and deal with fatigue and tiredness while maintaining concentration and race position.

When to use: All year round, particularly pre-season.

Description
- Warm up steadily and gradually to 80–85 per cent of maximum heart rate (MHR). Attempt to maintain race position throughout the session.
- Maintain this percentage HR for 40min with rpm of 85–100. You will almost certainly need to change gears to maintain this heart rate, particularly when using this session to start.

Variations
Be aware of the onset of fatigue, and don't immediately give in and change down a gear as you start to become tired. Accept that tiredness will hit you, and try to maintain HR and rpm until it is no longer possible.

CYCLE SESSION 4

Session objective: To extend the anaerobic threshold

Another demanding session, but one that has paid dramatic dividends with triathletes who have persevered with it. It teaches tolerance of discomfort, and a returning to that discomfort. A drop in time of over 10min for an Olympic distance cycle discipline has been accomplished with 'novice' cyclists and triathletes from one season to the next.

*   This session, like many, is best done on the turbo trainer.

Aim: To accept increasing discomfort.

When to use: All year round, particularly pre-season.

Description

*   Warm up to 75 per cent of MHR.
*   Ease back 10 beats per min (bpm) (allow to drop from, say, 160 to 150 bpm).
*   Go into large chainring and/or bigger gear as appropriate, and hold 100 rpm until bpm gets to 85 per cent of MHR, and maintain this effort for 30sec.
*   Change into small ring until HR drops to 70 per cent of MHR.
*   Repeat ten times or until HR will not return to 70 per cent of MHR in less than 3min.

Helen Jenkins of Great Britain has developed into an excellent cyclist by dint of pure hard training.

CYCLE SESSION 5

Session objective: Learning to deal with progressive resistance and increasing demand

There are similarities with the previous session, but this one is possibly even more demanding. The resistance (bigger gear) is increased with each repetition.

Aim: Dealing with pain and hurt...and then hurt a little bit more.

When to use: Particularly pre-season, and during the season when there are no important races.

Description
- Warm up to 75 per cent of MHR, then ease back to 70 per cent.
- Go into large chainring (assume 52 teeth) and 20-tooth sprocket. The session is based on assuming a gearing/sprocket size of 13-14-15-16-18-20-22).
- Stay in this gearing at 90–100 rpm until HR is 80 per cent of MHR.
- Go into small chainring until HR drops to 70 per cent of MHR.
- Into 52 × 18 at 90–100 rpm until 80 per cent of MHR is reached.
- Recover to 70 per cent of MHR.
- Into 52 × 17 at 90–100 rpm until 85 per cent of MHR is reached, then recover as before.
- 85 per cent of MHR in 52 × 16
- 90 per cent of MHR in 52 × 15
- 90 per cent of MHR in 52 × 14
- 95 per cent of MHR in 52 × 13
- Warm-down

Variations
You could use different percentages of MHR, or a different choice of gearing, both dependent on the athlete's state of fitness.

CYCLE SESSION 6

Session objective: Learning speed endurance and to cope with increasing demand

This session works on increasing the heart rate, and increasing effort over a substantial time period. It can simulate the feelings, hurt and discomfort of a non-drafting cycle section of an Olympic distance triathlon, or a 25-mile time trial. Many athletes never really dig deep into their reserves, but this session can teach that very quickly! It gives an appreciation of just how much more is there when superficial levels of effort have been reached.

Aim: To learn to hurt.

When to use: All year, more so pre-season, and during the race season when not racing at the weekend.

Description
- Warm up to 70–75 per cent of MHR.
- Into the large chainring; pedal at 80 per cent of MHR for 25min in the appropriate gear at 90–100 rpm.
- Without resting, go up one gear and hold for 20min at 85 per cent MHR.
- As before, go up one gear and hold for 15min at 90 per cent MHR.

Variations
Vary the choice of gears; aim for a lower heart rate if not fit.

Hard training means that you can ride hard during races.

CYCLE SESSION 7

Session objective: Extend anaerobic threshold, increasing demand, cadence

This session works on gradually increasing demand for effort with limited recovery.

Aim: To simulate race needs.

When to use: All year, particularly pre-season and during the race season when not racing at the weekend.

Description
- Warm up for 10min, then try to work at just five beats below your anaerobic threshold throughout (apart from recoveries, of course!). Attempt 100/110 rpm.
- The set is as follows:

30sec hard, 20sec spin recovery
40sec hard, 20sec spin recovery
50sec hard, 20sec spin recovery
60sec hard, 20sec spin recovery
70sec hard, 20sec spin recovery
80sec hard, 20sec spin recovery
90sec hard, 20sec spin recovery
1min 40sec hard, 20sec spin recovery
1min 50sec hard, 20sec spin recovery
2min hard
Spin for 5min and repeat

- Warm-down 10min.

Variations
Increase the two sets to three or more depending on fitness, experience and race distance.

CYCLE SESSION 8

Session objective: Achieving smoothness and cadence

Aim: To improve economy of effort, smoothness and cadence. Also to ensure that each leg will respond to the same degree.

When to use: Off season, but also whenever there's a feeling of losing smoothness.

Description
Have two chairs or something similar, one on each side of the bike to rest each leg on.

* Warm-up 10min.
* Take the left leg out of the pedal and work the right leg only for 30sec (rest the left leg on the chair). Try to make the action as smooth as possible, with particular attention to the dead spots at the top and bottom of the pedal stroke.
* Repeat with the left leg (resting the right leg on the chair).
* Go to 1min using both legs.
* Repeat each leg for 60sec, then 90sec, then 2min, all with 1min in between, and then come back down. 90, 60 and 30sec, still with 1min both legs working together after each set.
* Warm-down 10min.

Variations
Increase to two sets. If particularly weak, drop to 20, 40, 60 and 80sec for each repetition.

CYCLE SESSION 9

Session objective: Coping with very fast cadence and also the use of big gears

Aim: To improve economy of effort, smoothness and cadence. Also to ensure that you are able to deal with race needs and are happy with fast cadence and 'pushing'.

When to use: Pre-season seems to be effective, but also during the off season, particularly if there is a weakness in either area.

Description
- Warm-up 10min.
- Alternate 1min only at whatever gear you can hold 130 rpm, with your biggest gear (52 × 13?) where you have to pedal and ride smoothly, sitting down. Take 1min recovery between reps, and repeat six times on each gear.
- Warm-down 10min.

Variations
Number of repetitions, either decrease or increase. Possibly split into sets.

If enough hard work is done in cycle training, it means that the legs and lungs will be strong for the run.

CYCLE SESSION 10

Session objective: Increasing demand with endurance

Aim: To work on bigger gearing progressively while maintaining cadence; to sustain cadence/rpm with increased resistance.

When to use: All year as needed. The session can be effective during the racing season when there has been emphasis on pushing big gears to the detriment of rpm/cadence.

Description
- Start in your smallest gear (42 × 21/23) and work for 8min at 110 rpm, then
- go straight into the next gear up (42 × 19?) and work for 7min, then
- into 42 × 18 and work for 6min.
- Maintain this progress/pattern and increase right up to 42 × 13,
as in:

42 × 17, 5min
42 × 16, 4min
42 × 15, 3min
42 × 14, 2min
42 × 13, 1min
Try to maintain at least 100 rpm right the way through.

- Warm-down 10min.

Variations
Repeat the set, or repeat but in reverse order.

CYCLE SESSION 11

Session objective: Increasing demand with endurance

Aim: To work on bigger gearing progressively while maintaining cadence; to sustain cadence/rpm with increased resistance.

When to use: As the previous session, all year as needed.

Description
- Start in your smallest gear (42 × 21/23) and work for 2min at 110 rpm, then...
- go straight into the next gear up (42 × 19) and work for 2min, then...
- into 42 × 18 and work for 2min.
- Maintain this progress/pattern and increase right up to 42 × 13,

as in:

42 × 17, 2min
42 × 16, 2min
42 × 15, 2min
42 × 14, 2min
42 × 13, 2min

Try to maintain at least 100 rpm right the way through. Then comes the sting:

- Go directly into the big chainring and start again at 52 × 23 holding 2min right through to 52 × 13.

- Warm-down 10min.

Variations
Repeat the first part of the set (in the small, 42-teeth ring), or repeat all.

CYCLE SESSION 12

Session objective: To simulate hill climbing

The triathlete who is weak on hills is at a distinct disadvantage.

Increasing time is spent out of the saddle on each succeeding repetition, with the recovery time remaining the same. This makes the session far more taxing than working for the same repetition time.

- This session is best done on a turbo trainer.

Aim: To improve the ability to climb hills well.

When to use: All year.

Description
- Warm up.
- Then select 'hill' mode on turbo (or, of course, use outside hills!) or go into 52 × 13 (or biggest gear available) and pedal flat out for 1min, out of the saddle.
- Recover for 1min in easy gear.
- As before in 52 × 13, but hold for 2min.
- Recover for 1min.
- Repeat for 3, 4, 5min, maintaining 1min recovery only.

Variations
- Set appropriate resistance on turbos with that facility, rather than having to use biggest gearing.
- Stay in the saddle.
- Stay out of the saddle.
- Increase to 2, 3, 4, 5, 6min effort, and so on.

CYCLE SESSION 13

Session objective: Extended speed and power.

Aim: To learn to cope with increasing demand after initial fatigue; to maintain speed and power as fatigue increases.

When to use: Off season, pre-season.

Description
- Warm up with 10min spin.
- 10 repetitions of 52 × 13 for 1min aiming at race cadence, or 100 rpm if unsure.
- 1min recovery between efforts.
- 3min spin recovery in easy gear.
- 10min at 52 × 15 aiming at race cadence, or 100 rpm if unsure.
- 3min spin recovery in easy gear.
- 1min at 52 × 13, aiming at race cadence, or 100 rpm if unsure.
- 1min recovery.
- 2min at 52 × 13, aiming at race cadence, or 100 rpm if unsure.
- 1min recovery.
- 3min at 52 × 13, aiming at race cadence, or 100 rpm if unsure.
- Warm-down spin for 10min.

Variations
- Change gearing as appropriate.
- Repeat set for longer-distance triathletes.

CYCLE SESSION 14

Session objective: Adapting to pushing big gears, while trying to maintain a reasonable cadence

Aim: To maintain cadence in big gears, so you can run efficiently off the bike.

When to use: All year round, with some caution; pre-season recommended.

Description
- Warm up 10min at 100 rpm.
- 52 × 13 for 1min at 27/28mph or max HR less 20 beats, then straight into…
- 1min at 110 rpm in whatever gear needed to maintain speed or HR, then straight into…
- 52 × 13 for 2min at 27/28mph or max HR less 20 beats, then straight into…
- 2min at 110 rpm in whatever gear needed to maintain speed or HR, then straight into…
- 52 × 13 for 3min at 27/28mph or max HR less 20 beats, then straight into…
- 3min at 110 rpm in whatever gear needed to maintain speed or HR.
- Recover 2min, and repeat.

Variations
- Adjustment of gearing and speed depending on fitness and experience.
- Repeat one extra time; not recommended to repeat more than three times in all.

Non Stanford demonstrates great climbing ability.

CYCLE SESSION 15

Session objective: To improve the ability to climb long, sapping hills

This is a prolonged hill session, all done in the hardest gear that can be handled (usually 52 × 13); if using a turbo trainer with a percentage hill resistance, use it accordingly.

Aim: To develop the ability to withstand long climbs.

When to use: Off-season.

Description
- Warm up by going through the gears progressively for 2min each.
- Spin for 5min.
- Now a 30min hill endurance session:

1min out of the saddle followed by 1min sitting
2min out of the saddle followed by 2min sitting
3min out of the saddle followed by 3min sitting
4min out of the saddle followed by 4min sitting
5min out of the saddle followed by 5min sitting

- Spin for 10min.

Variations
- Adjust gearing and hill percentage incline, depending on fitness and experience.
- Take 1min rest between each succeeding climb if necessary.

CYCLE SESSION 16

Session objective: Learning to cope with progressive difficulty and increasing demand

Aim: To deal with increased demand.

When to use: Off season and some pre-season.

Description
Each repetition becomes longer, and each gear choice harder, so the difficulty is doubly increased, making this a tough session. However, once halfway is achieved it becomes more manageable.

- Warm up by going through gears progressively for 2min each, on the small ring (42) only. Then change up to the big ring and follow the programme:

52 × 22 for 1min
52 × 20 for 1min, recovery 52 × 22 for 1min
52 × 18 for 2min, recovery 52 × 22 for 1min
52 × 16 for 3min, recovery 52 × 22 for 1min
52 × 15 for 4min, recovery 52 × 22 for 1min
52 × 14 for 5min, recovery 52 × 22 for 1min
52 × 13 for 6min, recovery 52 × 22 for 1min
52 × 13 for 1min, recovery 52 × 22 for 1min
52 × 14 for 2min, recovery 52 × 22 for 1min
52 × 15 for 3min, recovery 52 × 22 for 1min
52 × 16 for 4min, recovery 52 × 22 for 1min
52 × 18 for 5min, recovery 52 × 22 for 1min
52 × 20 for 6min, recovery 52 × 22 for 1min

- Spin for 10min.

Variations
You can vary the times and recoveries.

CYCLE SESSION 17

Session objective: To maintain speed and cadence under pressure

Aim: To increase time on efforts while maintaining speed and cadence; to cope with repeated increasing demand.

When to use: Particularly pre-season.

Description
- Warm up for 10min in a gear that you can work up to 100 rpm.
- Go into a gear that you can hold 100 rpm at racing speed plus 10 per cent (so if your time for 25 miles is 1hr 15min, that is a speed of 20mph; your target is to train at 22mph for this session).

- 1min at this speed at 100 rpm; recovery spin for 1min easy gear.
- 2min at this speed at 100 rpm; recovery spin for 1min easy gear.
- 3min at this speed at 100 rpm; recovery spin for 1min easy gear.
- Spin for 3min.
- Repeat twice more.
- Warm-down spin for 10min.

Variations
Increase sets of repetitions to four, possibly five depending on fitness.

Even in a draft legal race, the athletes have to work individually for much of the time.

CYCLE SESSION 18

Session objective: To maintain race speed after initial fast start

It is often necessary to go out very hard on the cycle discipline after transition to move away from a forming pack or to catch up time lost on the swim. The ability to deal with that initial fatigue is an essential skill.

Aim: To cope with repeated increasing demand: race speed after initial fast burst.

When to use: All year, pre-season, possibly some during season.

Description
- Warm up for 10min in a gear that you can work up to 100 rpm.
- Go into biggest gear (52 × 13) flat out/100 per cent for 1min.
- 1min spin recovery, into…
- 6min at race pace plus 5 per cent, holding 100rpm.
- Spin 3min, and repeat five further times.
- Warm-down spin for 10min.

Variations
- Drop the 1min spin between the 1 and 6min effort.
- Increase the 1min spin recovery.
- Make the 6min effort shorter.
- Decrease the number of repetitions.

CYCLE SESSION 19

Session objective: Learning to change gears quickly when appropriate, and to maintain speed under pressure

Aim: To cope with gear changes under pressure, and the variation on gearing between 100 rpm and the 'big' gears.

When to use: All year, including race season when appropriate.

Detailed description
- Warm up for 10min in a gear that you can work up to 100 rpm.
- Go into big gear (52 × 13) for 5min at 5–10 per cent faster than race pace; then…
- directly into 1min at 110 rpm in whatever gear needed to maintain same speed and intensity.
- Recover 2 to 3min, then…
- 5min at 110 rpm at same speed/intensity; then…
- straight into big gear (52 × 13) for 1min maintaining same speed/intensity.
- Spin recovery for 3min, and repeat.
- Warm-down spin for 10min.

Variations
Increase sets of repetitions to three, possibly four for half Ironman® race distances.

Pure power on a bike is essential.

CYCLE SESSION 20

Session objective: To push/ increase the anaerobic threshold

This session is classic interval training.

When to use: All year, including the race season, when appropriate.

Description
- Warm up for 10min in a gear that you can work up to 100 rpm.
- Select challenging gearing that will require you to work hard to maintain 100 rpm.
- 1min in this gear at 100 rpm, then…
- 1min recovery spin in smaller chainring.
- Repeat until twenty repetitions done.
- Warm-down spin for 10min.

Variations
- Split into two sets of ten repetitions.
- Drop the number of repetitions to ten or fifteen.
- Increase the number of repetitions to thirty.

CYCLE SESSION 21

Session objective: To push the anaerobic threshold

Classic interval training, extended time period.

Aim: To increase the aerobic and anaerobic threshold, and race speed.

When to use: All year, though less so in the race season.

Description
- Warm up for 10min in a gear that you can work up to 100 rpm.
- Select gearing that you will need to maintain 100 rpm.
- 15min in this gear at 100 rpm, aiming for current race speed plus 10 per cent; therefore if you race at 20mph, train this session at 22mph.

CYCLE SESSION 21 (continued)

- 3min spin recovery, easy gear.
- Repeat three more times until four repetitions done.
- Warm-down spin for 10min.

Variations
- Split into three sets of 20min.
- Increase the number of repetitions to five.

CYCLE SESSION 22

Session objective: Improve race speed under pressure, ability to move away from a pack

Aim: Ability to increase speed at will when necessary, and to increase power/wattage from basic speed.

When to use: Pre-season and race season.

Description
- Steady warm-up for 10min, going through the gears.
- 1min at race speed at 100 rpm.
- At the end of the 1min, go up directly three gears and push flat out, maintaining race position.
- Recover 3min spin in easy gear.
- Repeat four more times until five repetitions done.
- Warm-down spin for 10min.

Variations
- Maximum of ten repetitions.
- Go up only two gears, depending on fitness.

CYCLE SESSION 23

Session objective: Sustained power and speed

Aim: To improve ability to maintain top power and speed when fatigued; increasing power over a sustained period of time.

When to use: All year, particularly pre-season and sometimes race season.

Description

- Steady warm-up for 10min, going through gears. Then…
- three bursts of 30sec at fast turnover.
- 4min at flat-out speed; biggest gear you can hold to maintain 90+ rpm.
- Spin recovery, easy gear for at least 4min, up to as much as 6min if needed.
- Repeat three further times.
- Warm down at least 10min, preferably 15min, to include three sets of 100 rpm in very easy gear.

Variations

Appropriate gearing only.

Speed when cornering on the bike can be maintained if worked on during training.

CYCLE SESSION 24

Session objective: To sustain race speed under continuous pressure

The entire session of one hour is done at race pace or faster.

Aim: Ability to revise race speed and maintain it.

When to use: All year, particularly pre-season, and sometimes in the race season if appropriate.

Description
- Steady warm-up for 10min, going through the gears.
- 2min at 5 per cent faster than current Olympic distance race speed, into...
- 2min at current Olympic distance race speed, into...
- 90sec at 10 per cent faster than current Olympic distance race speed, into...
- 90sec at current Olympic distance race speed, into...
- 60sec at 15 per cent faster than current Olympic distance race speed, into...
- 60sec at current Olympic distance race speed, into...
- 30sec at 20 per cent faster than current Olympic distance race speed, into...
- 30sec at current Olympic distance race speed, then...
- immediately into repetition of above, and then...
- repeat once more for three repetitions in all.
- 3min spin, then...
- repeat the above session twice through.
- 3min spin, then...
- repeat the above session once through.
- Warm down at least 10min spinning.

Variations
For experienced and/or extremely fit triathletes, go through a set of four, then three, then two, and finally one repetition for ten sets in all rather than six.

CYCLE SESSION 25

Session objective: Maintaining speed when fatigued

Aim: To maintain the same speed with decreasing recovery.

When to use: All year, particularly pre-season, and sometimes in the race season if appropriate.

Description
- Steady warm-up for 10min, going through the gears.
- 30sec at race pace plus 10/20 per cent: if your race speed averages 20mph, then this session is done at between 22 and 24mph:

30sec spin recovery
30sec at race pace plus 10/20 per cent
25sec spin recovery
30sec at race pace plus 10/20 per cent
20 sec spin recovery
30sec at race pace plus 10/20 per cent
15sec spin recovery
30sec at race pace plus 10/20 per cent
10sec spin recovery
30sec at race pace plus 10/20 per cent
5sec spin recovery

- then immediately back into the entire series of repetitions without any extra recovery…
- and then repeat once more!
- Spin recovery 3 to 5min, then…
- repeat series for second time.
- Spin recovery 3 to 5min, then…
- repeat series for third time.
- Warm down at least 10min spinning.

In essence, nine sets of reducing recovery are done in this session.

Variations
No variations: if the session feels 'easy', then set the speed higher.

CYCLE SESSION 26

Session objective: Ironman® and half Ironman® simulation, extended quality

- This session is best done on a turbo trainer (though it can be done on the road) for mental strength in addition to physical.

A three-hour session that is both physically and mentally demanding for longer-distance triathletes; a combination of extended speed time-trialling, strength and power, intended to simulate race conditions.

Aim: The ability to train/race hard without a warm-up, thereby simulating race conditions.

When to use: Off season (primarily the second half of the off season and the immediate pre-season).

Description
- No warm-up; straight into…
- 1hr at best race time-trial speed, into…
- 5min spin recovery, into…
- 55min of hill repetitions (either with the hill incline facility, or in the biggest gear [53 × 13]) as 2, 3, 4, 5, 6min out of the saddle with just 1min spin recovery, and then…
- repeat set. If necessary take a few minutes spin after the first 6min effort, then into…
- 5min spin recovery, into…
- 55min of anaerobic threshold work, suggested 6 × 6min at just faster than 25 time-trial race pace with 1min spin recovery.

Variations
- For half Ironman® , this session is longer than racing time: mentally it will make the half Ironman® athlete very confident.
- Use a shorter time: 60, 90min, 2hr with appropriate shorter 'effort' times.
- Stay in the saddle on hill repeats.

CYCLE SESSION 27

Session objective: Sustaining speed when tired

When to use: All year, particularly pre-season.

Description
Hill-climbing repetitions followed by hard effort. Often in a race situation there is a tendency to fall off speed after a hard effort (such as hill climbing).

*   Hill repetitions for 1hr, followed immediately by...
*   a flat 1hr in race position.
*   Hill climb for a set period/distance, say 3min/800m...
*   hill descend as recovery, and...
*   repeat for one hour.
*   Immediately after the final climb, go straight into...
*   a 1hr time trial.

Variations
*   Less time distance on hills and effort (perhaps for a sprint distance or when recovering from injury).
*   Variation on time for hills: 1, 2, 4, 5, 6min efforts, depending on weaknesses.
*   Longer time trial after hills (perhaps for half Ironman®).
*   Stay in the saddle.
*   Stay out of the saddle.

CYCLE SESSION 28

Session objective: Working on strength when tired after speed

When to use: All year, particularly pre-season.

Description
This session is effectively a reverse of the previous session: a hard time-trial effort followed by hill-climbing repetitions. Again, in a race situation there is a tendency to lack strength for climbing after a flat time-trial effort.

- A flat 1hr in race position.
- Hill repetitions for 1hr, followed immediately by...
- hill climbs for a set period/distance, say 3mins/800m, then...
- hill descend as recovery.
- Repeat for one hour.
- Immediately after time trial go straight into a hill-climb effort.

Variations
- Less time distance on hills and effort (perhaps for sprint distance or when recovering from injury).
- Variation on time for hills: 1, 2, 4, 5, 6min efforts, depending on weaknesses.
- Longer/shorter hills after time-trial effort.
- Stay in the saddle.
- Stay out of the saddle.

CYCLE SESSION 29

Session objective: Power and sprint speed. To promote the ability to move away immediately when in danger of being caught in a 'drafting' situation

Aim: Short sprint sessions will improve the ability and efficiency to increase speed quickly when necessary.

When to use: Off season (primarily second half of the off season and immediate pre-season).

- This session is best and most safely done on a turbo trainer.

Description
- Warm up gradually, increasing speed to around 65/70 per cent of maximum heart rate.
- Go into the biggest gear possible, between 52 × 13 and 52 × 17 (choose as appropriate), and go flat out for 5sec only.
- Recover for 10sec only, and…
- repeat the effort.

After three to four sprint efforts, HR should be at approximately 85 per cent max and will remain constant at this level. However, if HR does rise significantly higher than this, increase the recovery time. The sprint efforts must remain at 5sec only, and under no circumstances should exceed 8sec.

- Warm up
- Sprint flat out (big gear) for 5sec
- Recover 10sec only
- Repeat above ten times
- Easy recovery for 1min
- Repeat all above so that 40 × 5sec sprints are done in all

Although the efforts are very short, the above is an extremely demanding session as the HR doesn't have very much time to decrease in the 10sec recovery intervals.

Variations
- Beginners may wish to start with 5 × 5sec and repeat three times or similar.
- Most accurate efforts and recoveries are achieved by using a pre-set interval timer set at the appropriate times.

CYCLE SESSION 30

Session objective: Extended power and sprint speed

Although age-group racing is largely non-drafting, there are often occasions when it is necessary to 'get away' from a pack, usually when triathletes of similar ability have exited the swim together and unconsciously formed into a 'loose' pack. That ability to sprint can prevent an athlete being penalized for drafting.

Aim: Longer sprint sessions will improve the ability and efficiency to maintain and/or increase speed when passing another cyclist/triathlete during the race.

When to use: Immediate pre-season and mid-season.

- This session is best and most safely done on a turbo trainer.

Description
- Warm up.
- Select gear which is slightly 'too big' (you should feel as if you are having to make an effort to handle this gear).
- Sprint flat out for 15sec.
- Recover to 70 per cent max HR.
- Repeat ten times.

For both sprint sessions, as efforts are analactic/anaerobic, the HR will continue to rise after 15sec efforts for a short time. This is to be expected and should not be a matter for concern.

Variations
Beginners may wish to start with 5 × 15sec, and repeat twice.

PART III
RUNNING

CHAPTER 6

RUNNING TECHNIQUE

Good technique is crucial in running during a triathlon, as the athlete is coming into the final discipline already fatigued from swimming and cycling. The technique of any endurance running is modified sprinting, but the action of running has to be efficient to lessen any unnecessary use of energy.

The Running Action

Running consists of a propulsive phase and a recovery phase. The propulsive phase starts as soon as the foot makes contact with the ground during a running stride. The whole of the bodyweight is impacted upon the foot as the hips and trunk are moved forwards over the foot, and the hip, knee and ankle stretch out.

The recovery phase begins with the foot leaving the ground. The foot is pulled upwards and the thigh swings forwards and through until it is almost parallel to the ground. The lower part of the leg then comes forwards as the thigh begins to move downwards. The whole leg then sweeps backwards and downwards until the foot strikes the ground again.

The upper body remains upright or leaning slightly forwards. Energy can be wasted by getting away from forward, horizontal progress by lifting and dropping the head and hips. By always thinking of keeping the hips up high, we avoid the body sagging down, particularly as we get progressively more tired, and this avoids having to use valuable energy to lift the body back up again.

The arm action matches the leg action, the left arm coming forwards at the same time as the right leg comes forwards, and vice versa, in an equal and opposite action and reaction. The arm movement should be kept relaxed and rhythmic, moving backwards and forwards in a straight line with the hands loosely cupped and the thumbs resting on the fingers. A powerful, strong arm-drive will dictate how fast the legs move and the length of stride. Leg speed (cadence) is absolutely critical for fast running and a good, strong arm action will ensure this. Just as a good leg kick in swimming is important for balance and maintaining a good position, so is a strong upper body and arm drive in running.

Any sideways arm movement will detract from the economy of running. The arms balance and drive the legs, so the arms should swing forwards and back rather than sideways. The arm action should be economical and relaxed, but the speed and height of the arm swing (particularly on the back swing) contributes to cadence, and hence running speed.

Experienced runners check their action and body position frequently, particularly the head position, upright running, cadence and foot strike.

Hip and lower body mobility will also influence the speed and efficiency of running. Poor mobility will inhibit stride length. Good running technique involves the flexion and extension and some rotation of the ankle, knee and hip. In running:

- Speed = stride length × stride rate

If we wish to improve either of these factors, then we must increase the range of movement in the joints and the strength in the running muscle groups.

The Effects of Cycling on Running

In the early stages of triathlon running, cycling will have a big impact on the speed of running. In cycling, the legs have been circling continually at around 80 to 100 revolutions per minute (rpm), and there has been no impact on the ground. As the run discipline starts, that circular movement becomes an up-and-down one, with impact and jarring on each step. The impact of each step can multiply bodyweight by as much as four times.

Even with experienced runners, running after cycling can be challenging and difficult. It is important that the cycling cadence is not too slow (often caused by using too big a gear), as muscle memory will come into play. If the cadence on the bike section has been 60 or 70 rpm, rather than 80 to 100 rpm, then that cadence will be remembered when the run starts and the athlete will run at that leg speed. Indications are that successful fast running requires a leg turnover or cadence of at least 160 per minute (both left and right legs). Dividing the 160 strike rate by two, this equates nicely with the 80 to 100 rpm cycle cadence. Therefore selecting too big a gear on the cycling phase may have a negative effect on running speed.

Good Technique Versus Poor Technique

Good technique will lead to economy of effort, and a good runner will have an upright running action, a steady head position looking forwards and level, a high knee lift, a good stride length, a foot strike towards the front of the foot, a fast stride frequency (180 foot touches plus per minute of running), and the ability to maintain that stride frequency throughout the run. An upright running action can be helped by thinking of cotton attached to the head and pulling up, by pushing the hips forwards, and by leaning forwards from the feet.

In addition a runner with good technique will avoid tense or tight shoulders and neck, as this will contribute to early fatigue.

Breathing should be controlled: holding the breath or very shallow breathing will also lead to early fatigue. This can be controlled by focusing on breathing *out* rather than on breathing *in*.

An emphasis on keeping the hips forwards and high will ensure that stride length is good. Dropped hips are caused either by cumulative fatigue from the cycle discipline, or weak core muscles.

Conversely, a poor runner will have a seated running action, the body bobbing up and down, an unsteady head position with the eyes looking down rather than forwards and level, the hips dropped, the backside stuck out, a low knee lift, an over-long or very short stride length, a heel strike with the foot under or behind the knee, a low stride frequency (fewer than 140 foot touches per minute), and a slowing of stride frequency as fatigue becomes apparent.

Heel striking is associated with overstriding. It creates a braking effect, as the body's centre of gravity will be behind the foot strike each time. A tremendous amount of energy is then required to bring the bodyweight back in front – basically a 'lift' each stride. Impact injuries are also frequent with an overlong stride length. Leaning back rather than forwards will also contribute to the braking effect.

To summarize, it is important to beware of the following:

- **Over-striding:** braking effect on each stride – it breaks the momentum of each stride
- **Seated running:** hips back, bum out
- **Tight shoulders:** no neck, shoulders tense and tight
- **Forced breathing:** shallow breathing, holding the breath, causing early fatigue – try very deep, belly breathing, and focus on breathing out rather than in
- **Tight/incorrect head position:** a rolling, bobbing head detracts from the run technique; it is important to focus on the ground 15–20ft in front, to lift the head occasionally, and relax the lower jaw. Practise on fast runs as well as easy
- **Heel strike:** involves a foot strike under the knee; bobbing up and down while running
- **Uneven arm action**

Conversely, it is important to emphasize the beneficial effects of the following:

- **Upright running** – remember the cotton attached to the head and pulling up, pushing the hips forwards, and leaning forwards from the feet
- **Improved stride frequency** – 90+, and maintaining a good cadence on all runs
- **A shorter stride**
- **Even arm action**

Textbook qualities would be a good knee lift, good stride length, and to maintain speed of stride.

Be aware of different surfaces, and the extra fatigue induced by cycling.

Running Drills

Running drills isolate the individual aspects of the running action. They require coordination and balance, and are carried out for very short distances to avoid fatigue when technique may break down. The most important parts of the running action are:

- high lift of the upper leg
- paw down and pull back of the lead leg
- full extension and lift of the rear leg
- full range of arm movement

For the legs and feet progressively the sequence is toe up, heel up, knee up, reach out, claw back.

Running drills may not seem to be as important as swimming drills. However, running is the final discipline, when tiredness has already set in, and the importance of practising running drills will ensure that run technique is maintained even through that fatigue. By working hard on running drills, the usual range of movement will be extended and the likelihood is that foot strike will be more powerful.

As running is a high-impact activity, running on grass is advisable in the early stages of running drills. Impact and the chance of soreness and injury will be reduced by training on a softer surface.

Skipping
A simple activity such as skipping is a good warm-up that will also need some coordination. Gradually increasing the height of each skip will require more and more leg strength, and this basic activity will supply two of the essential needs for running; coordination and leg power.

Lunges

Improving mobility will ensure that the stride length during the run will be increased without having to resort to heel-striking and the accompanying 'braking' effect. Lunges will improve mobility and will also have an effect on leg strength. A lunge is basically a very long step forwards while keeping the upper body upright and lowering the hips towards the floor (the back leg knee shouldn't touch the floor). This lunge stretches the muscles in the upper legs and backside, and also strengthens these areas when the rear leg is pulled forwards and upwards into the next step or lunge. Each lunge should be held for a count of two.

Heel Flicks

Speed of stride is the single most important factor in fast running, and practising the heel flicks drill emphasizes the necessary speed of stride. The drill involves running with very short strides and flicking the heels upwards to try to make contact with the gluteus muscles (backside). It is important to emphasize the speed of the flick-ups while main-taining the upper leg from hip to knee perpendicular to the floor. There should be further emphasis on having as little 'resting' contact with the ground as possible: as soon as the foot makes contact with the ground, it should be lifted.

- **Teaching/coaching point:** Visualize the ground as 'electrified' and if the feet are in contact for more than one tenth of a second, an electric shock follows!

The 1, 2, Flick Drill

A progression in the heel flick drill is to combine two running steps followed by one heel flick-up: the 1, 2, flick drill. This variation of two short, fast strides followed by a flick-up as the third stride requires and emphasizes good coordination, and it may be necessary to practise it by walking it in the early stages of learning it.

Rapid Foot Movement

Working on rapid foot movement is one of the most important aspects for fast running: a fast cadence is essential. Take very short steps pushing off from the ground with the toes pointing downwards and barely lifting from the ground; this must be performed as fast as possible for twenty to thirty repetitions. Then open up the stride and run out.

High Knee Drill

This drill is used to lift the knees and open up the running stride, but also to work further on rapid foot and leg movement, reducing the amount of time spent in contact with the ground (as described above): any extra ground contact time absorbs energy and should be avoided.

Concentration is needed to focus on both aspects. The knees are brought up high by bounding upwards with each stride and foot contact. It is important to maintain good overall running technique with this drill, and not lean backwards as the knees come up: looking forwards and slightly upwards will help with this. The speed of performing the high knee drill can be gradually increased as confidence is gained, and the power and drive of the arms should also be increased as the drill progresses.

Ballet Kick or Kick Through

With the bodyweight taken on one leg, the other leg is kicked upwards to the opposite hand: thus with the weight on the left leg, the straight right leg kicks up to the left hand. The weight-bearing leg is raised on to the toes for a greater range of mobility. This drill is best practised slowly initially by walking it through to maintain good coordination, before going through more quickly. It is important to emphasize 'light feet'.

Sideways Running (Crossover Drill)

Running sideways with the legs crossing in front and behind each other may seem easy, but if coordination is a problem, this drill is effective. A gradual progression with speed of movement coupled with using the arms as a counter balance will create good coordination.

Summary of Running Drills

Heel flicks:
More rapid contact with the ground
Faster flick-ups (as hard as possible, but not moving forwards very far)

1, 2, flick:
Alternate flick-up every three strides, coordination drill ensures you move the arms
Focus on coordination, and again, don't try to move forwards too fast

High knees:
Drive with the arms … jog at the end
Increase speed of movement and intensity

Rapid foot movement:
Short, 'machine gun' very close, then run out
Run tall, don't lift the feet too high, little/no noise

Kick through:
One step, two step, then straight leg kick-up to the opposite hand
The support leg is on the ground, but raised on to the toes (giving greater range of mobility)
Do this by walking through to start, emphasize 'light feet'

High knee lift:
Lift knee, extend forwards, drop the foot back to underneath the knee, return to the floor just in front of the other foot
Then bring in the arms by raising the opposite arm as the knee is first lifted

Sideways crossover forwards and back
Use the arms to counterbalance
Then turn from this to running forwards

The Running Ladder

The running ladder or running squares can be an unfolded rope ladder on the floor, or a taped line of squares. The athlete aims to run a series of drills, placing a foot in each square. Leg speed is focused on here, and the drills above used (a focus on fast leg speed and strength exercises).

The running ladder is particularly helpful with new runners and triathletes, and those who have initial problems with coordination. Examples are one foot in each square, then speed up, then hop, then double foot jump every other square; alternate run and hop; double foot jumping in and out of square, then either side of square. Ensure that you land on the ball of the foot each time.

Strength and Power Exercises for Running

It may seem unlikely, but distance runners often have weak leg muscles. This is because, with a concentration on pure distance running, there is rarely time made during training for speed and power and strength work. However, it may be necessary to commit to power and strength training, particularly if there is a specific weakness. Exercises for strength and power are given below. Observe a degree of caution, however, particularly if such power training has not been done previously, because injury is possible if the exercises are hurried or not performed properly.

Two Foot Explosive Jumps

Rebound (on both feet together) very lightly on the spot, then explode into bringing both knees up towards your chest. Go back to rebounding, then repeat the explosive effort, this time with two explosive efforts. Repeat up to ten counts, or until tired. The arms must be used for balance and upward lift.

Single Foot Explosive Jumps

As above, but on one leg. This exercise is extremely fatiguing and should only be undertaken by strong, experienced athletes.

Hopping

Following on from the above exercise, there are a number of hopping exercises that will promote strength and power. Fast hopping with the strike over the mid-foot or ball of the foot will promote these. Always attempt to keep an upright posture with the hips forwards. Variations include:

- single foot hopping only
- alternating three hops on one foot, then three on the other foot
- alternating two hops and one stride (sometimes called 'Indian' hopping)
- alternating skipping and hopping

CHAPTER 7

RUN SESSIONS

Our thirty suggested and recommended running sessions divide into four very rough groups: endurance, interval training, hills and technique. The interval sessions are listed first, primarily because we suggest a 'starting point' from which to base times for repetitions. These are followed by endurance (the long runs), then hills and finally technique. However, no preferred importance is meant by this order.

What is important is to be totally realistic about your own strengths and weaknesses, and to choose sessions and train accordingly. It is a very human and normal triathlete failing to always choose to do the type of training session that we are good at, rather than work on our weaknesses!

Run session 1: The starting point
Run session 2: Improving 10km racing speed
Run session 3: Maintaining run speed when tired or under pressure
Run session 4: Maintaining racing speed under pressure
Run session 5: Mixed pace session
Run session 6: Maintaining leg speed during endurance running
Run session 7: 'Classic' anaerobic threshold session

Run session 8: Ironman® and half Ironman® running
Run session 9: Two-man parlaaf
Run session 10: Faster than race pace 400m
Run session 11: Repetition 2km
Run session 12: Increasing demand repetition 2km
Run session 13: Quality miles
Run session 14: Continuous alternate miles
Run session 15: Repetition 200m
Run session 16: Tempo and plus-tempo pace run
Run session 17: Maintenance of pace at start of run discipline
Run session 18: Speed, increasing demand on endurance
Run session 19: Speed
Run session 20: Interval plus sustained effort
Run session 21: The long run
Run session 22: The long run, out and back
Run session 23: The long run, increasing demand
Run session 24: The long run, paced and timed, progressive
Run session 25: Hill reps
Run session 26: Hill reps
Run session 27: Hill reps
Run session 28: Hill reps
Run session 29: Hill reps
Run session 30: Drills and techniques

RUN SESSION 1

Session objective: The starting point

Aim: To find the starting point of where you are in fitness, and to establish the times/distances/repetitions you should be aiming for.

When to use: Off season and pre-season.

Description
15min run at full effort. Be rested, prepared, take this session seriously.

We can use this session as an indicator for 'roughly' present 5km racing pace. Therefore 10km pace will be twice the time, and add 10 per cent (3min). In a dream time trial, 5km is covered and the 10km time is likely to be around 33min. If 4km is covered, then around 8km in 33min and so on. Re-test every six weeks or so.

Variations
If very unfit go for 12min rather than 15.

The three medallists at the 2012 London Olympic Games are also the three best runners in triathlon.

RUN SESSION 2

Session objective: Improving 10km racing speed

Aim: To achieve 10km race speed at present 5km race speed. The first 9min should be relatively comfortable. The second 9min is harder, but after a 90sec rest is acceptable. Then comes the sting in the tail by going at 5km race speed one more time and taking the total distance covered up to 7.5km.

When to use: Off season, and particularly pre-season.

Description
It is essential to know your best time for 5km for this session – for example, 18min.

- After warm-up, run half the distance (2.5km) in half the time (9min).
- Jog recovery for 90sec only.
- Repeat run half the distance (2.5km) in half the time (9min).
- Jog recovery for 90sec only.
- Third repetition of run half the distance (2.5km) in half the time (9min).

Variations
- As you get fitter and faster, decrease recovery between efforts to 1min only.
- For slower runners, outside 25min for 5km pace, stay at a maximum of 10min for the three repetitions, perhaps initially begin with 8min then 9, finally 10. Re-test 5km speed and adjust as necessary.

RUN SESSION 3

Session objective: Maintaining run speed when tired or under pressure

After getting a good start on the final discipline, the hard bit is maintaining that speed when you're getting more and more tired after the efforts on the swim, the bike and the start of the run. This run session seem to be particularly effective for this: it relies on decreasing recovery while holding race pace.

When to use: All year, but particularly pre-season.

Description
Work out your 200m training pace (approximately 10sec per 200m faster than your racing 10km pace); if you run 48–50min for the 10km, that's about 8min miling, which gives 400m in 2min; halve that for 200m to give 1min, and then take off the 10sec: so you're aiming at 50sec for each repetition.

- Warm up, then:
- Run the first 200m in 50sec: it should feel like a hard effort, but by no means flat out.
- Then jog for 90sec, then...
- repeat the 200m run and jog for 75sec, then...
- repeat the 200m again, this time jog for 60sec, then...
- run 200m, jog for 45sec
- run 200m, jog for 30sec
- run 200m, jog for 15sec
- run 200m....

After the last 200m effort, jog for 90sec and repeat the reducing recovery cycle again. And if you're still feeling in control, go through it again.

The first set through gives you seven 200m repetitions, then further sets give you six each time; going though the full three times makes nineteen repetitions.

Variations
Drop to two sets if you are coming back from injury or tired.

RUN SESSION 4

Session objective: Maintaining racing speed under pressure

Aim: To maintain faster than race pace. In this session 18min will have been run significantly faster than sprint-distance racing speed with a limited recovery.

When to use: Off season and pre-season, sometimes mid-season with discretion.

Description
- 1min run at between 1,500m and 3,000m race pace, 1min jog recovery.
- 2min run at between 1,500m and 3,000m race pace, 1min jog recovery.
- 3min run at between 1,500m and 3,000m race pace, 1min jog recovery.
- Jog for 3min after the 3min effort.
- Then repeat twice more.

In shorthand: 1, 2, 3min fast with 60sec recovery (+ 3 jog) × 3

Variations
- Start with two sets of repetitions.
- If very fit go up to four sets of repetitions.
- Add a 4min rep after the 3min each time.

Even in a 5k or 10k run discipline, sprinting is essential. Nicola Spirig and Lisa Norden at the London Olympic Games.

RUN SESSION 5

Session objective: Mixed pace session

Many runners (particularly triathletes) seem unwilling or unable to train at different speeds. Then when they race they are disappointed that they are not able to pick up the pace and be competitive. This session gives an appreciation of different pacing, and also how that different pace feels when you're already tired.

Aim: To achieve an appreciation of running at a variety of different speeds, and how that feels when tired.

When to use: All year, and can be used as a 'pick-up' during the racing season if/when there doesn't seem to be an improvement on run speed even when fit.

Description
* Warm up, then…
* 10min at 5km pace, 3min jog recovery
* 10 × 30sec at 800m pace, 30sec jog, 3min jog recovery.
* 1, 2, 3min at 1,500m pace with 1min jog recovery only.

Variations
* Vary, drop time for sprint distance to:

6, 7min at 3km/5km pace
Six to eight reps of 30sec
1, 1½, 2min at 1,500m pace

* Repeat full set (particularly for half Ironman®/longer distances)

RUN SESSION 6

Session objective: Maintaining leg speed (fast-twitch muscle memory) during endurance running

Aim: To keep an element of speed while building up stamina/endurance. It's very easy for the 'long' run to become an aimless shuffle, and this session focuses on thirty sections of leg speed. It also makes the session go much more quickly!

When to use: All year including off season.

Description
- Warm up for 10min, then…
- go into 30sec of fast running, say 85/90 per cent effort, then…
- ease back for 30sec as a steady run rather than a jog.
- Repeat ten times through.
- Jog 3min.
- Repeat above session twice more through.
- Warm down easy running 10min.

Variations
- 20sec of fast leg turnover with 40sec recovery to begin with, or when tired. 40sec of fast sections with 20sec recovery when fit and wanting to do a challenging session.
- 30min run with one set of 30/30 on/off.
- Increase number of repetitions.
- Increase number of sets.
- Increase total time for the session.

RUN SESSION 7

Session objective: 'Classic' anaerobic threshold session.

The exercise physiologists tell us that a 6min effort at race pace, repeated between four to eight times at racing speed with minimal recovery, will fulfil the needs of adaptation for racing speed.

For triathletes training on three disciplines, this fits in nicely with our programmes (overall on each discipline):

For swimming, 6 × 400m swim and rest 6min (or 6.30/7.00 etc).
For cycling, 6 × 6min on turbo, recovery 1min spin.
For running, 6 × 1 mile (or 1,500m, 1,200m etc), recovery 1min.

Aim: To extend anaerobic threshold, dealing with race pace fatigue.

When to use: All year.

Description
- Warm up, then (as above)
- 6 × 1 mile at just faster than 10km racing pace (5km pace, or 'dream' 10km race pace)…
- recovery 1min in between.

Variations
Don't start your training programme with 6 × 1 mile! To get to this level of fitness will take time and gradual improvement in fitness. Start at (maybe) 4 × ¾ mile with a 2min recovery, and gradually increase the distance and number of repetitions and decrease recovery time:

Step one: 4 × ¾ mile with 2min recovery.
Step two: 4 × ¾ mile with 90sec recovery.
Step three: 5 × ¾ mile with 90sec recovery.
Step four: 4 × 1 mile with 2min recovery.
Step five: 4 × 1 mile with 90sec recovery.

RUN SESSION 8

Session objective: Ironman® and half Ironman® running; 5km/marathon pace

Continuous 400m efforts are run at target 5km time, and target marathon time. A World Class Ironman® triathlete with a best 5km time of (say) 19min, and a target marathon time of 3hr, would aim to run consecutive 400m efforts at 90sec and 1min 45sec. The aim would be to run thirty (or more) consecutive 400m.

This gives a total of 12km with more than half of this distance, and therefore more than the 5km distance, at 5km racing pace. Being able to run the full 12km will depend on fitness. If the triathlete is not yet fit enough to do the full session in one go, then split into two (or more) sets of 400m, perhaps 18 × 400m, then 12 × 400m with a short recovery in between.

Aim: To improve marathon and half-marathon speed.

When to use: All year.

Description

- Warm up, then...
- 30 × 400m alternating 1.30/1.45

Variations
As above, split into two or more sets if injured, not fully fit, or generally fatigued.

RUN SESSION 9

Session objective: Two-man (woman) parlaaf

Aim: To promote speed endurance and mental toughness, race situation practice.

When to use: Throughout the year.

Description

This session is best done on a track, or an area with a 'jog across' section. It's a great session for working with a group with teams of two working against each other, highly motivational and can be extremely tough. One runner starts midway along the straight of a 400m track (or similar); his partner waits midway on the opposite straight. The first athlete runs 200m around the track and hands over to his partner; he then has to jog across the track to be in place for when his partner (second runner) arrives after completing his 200m effort. This pattern continues for as many as thirty repetitions. In a group or squad situation, the competitive instinct takes over and the session becomes very tough with athletes racing against each other. An excellent session for speed endurance and mental toughness.

In shorthand: Two-man parlaaf × 200m, jog across recovery

Variations
- Can be done with three team members and taking recovery as 'waiting' for your team member to come in, rather than jogging across.
- Variations on the distance of track to shorten the distance.
- Change in number of repetitions to reflect the state of fitness.

RUN SESSION 10

Session objective: Faster than race pace 400m

Aim: To improve strength and speed, to be aware of pace judgement, to develop mental toughness, and to be able to maintain race pace under pressure.

When to use: Some off season, predominantly pre-season, and occasionally during the season to sharpen up.

Description
A set of repetition 400m efforts, all based at 3,000m race pace, but with a sting in the tail. Ten 400m efforts are run at 3km race pace; the first three are run with just 20sec recovery between them, then there is a 1min recovery. The three are repeated, again with a 20sec recovery between, and a further 1min rest after all three. Finally a fourth 400m is attempted rather than three. The extra effort required for the extra 400m repetition makes this a very demanding session.

In shorthand: 10 × 400m as 3, 3, 4; 20sec recovery, 60sec after each sub-set.

Variations
The addition of two extra 400m, making the sub-sets three, then four, and finally five efforts for a total of twelve in all. Even more demanding!

RUN SESSION 11

Session objective: Repetition 2km

Aim: To improve strength and be aware of pace judgement.

When to use: Off season and pre-season.

Description
This session involves a 2km distance repeated five times. Mentally it is very tough to do repeats on longer distances, however for middle/long-distance running and triathlon, it is essential. The 2km should be repeated at faster than racing pace for 10km.

• It is recommended to do this repetition on trails rather than on the track

In shorthand: 5 × 2km (recovery 2min)

Variations
For sprint-distance triathletes, use repetitions of 1km, though keep recovery as 2min. Beginners over the Olympic distance should also start here. For experienced Olympic-distance triathletes the 5 × 1km session can be a useful speed-training session.

RUN SESSION 12

Session objective: Increasing demand, repetition of 2km

Aim: To improve strength, to be aware of pace judgement, to be able to respond to fast-finishing athletes, and to up your pace under pressure.

When to use: Off season and pre-season.

Description
A variation on the previous session, repetition 2km, but this time we look to up the pace each time. A little more recovery is needed here, so extend the 2min to 4 or 5min. The first repetition is at just faster than 10km pace, the second at 5km race pace, and the aim for the third is at 3km race pace. As above, mentally this is very tough.

- Again, it is recommended to do this session on trails or grass rather than on the track

In shorthand: 3 × 2km (recovery 4min)

Variations
- For sprint-distance triathletes, repetitions of 1km, recovery 4min. Beginners over the Olympic distance should also start here.
- For experienced Olympic-distance triathletes the 5 × 1km session can be a useful speed-training session.
- For experienced triathletes, increase the three repetitions to four.

RUN SESSION 13

Session objective: Quality speed repetitions

Aim: To improve sustained speed, to run faster.

When to use: Pre-season and during the race season.

Description
Four by 1 mile repetitions at 99 per cent maximum speed.

Just as it is important to run at 5km pace to improve your 10km time, and at 10km pace to improve half and full marathon time and performance, so it is equally important to train at 3,000m and even 1,500 and 800m pace to improve the performance of the distance above each one.

Training at a faster-than-race pace speed will develop better economy of effort, timing and coordination, and comfort while running fast. So, to achieve a good 10km time, the athlete has to bring the 5km time down; to run a good 5km, you'll need to bring the 3,000m time down, and equally the 1,500m time as well.

When training for speed and quality it is important to take sufficient recovery, since the aim here is to improve sustained speed.

In shorthand: 4 × 1 mile, recovery 5min

Variations
5 × 800m with 3 to 4min recovery.
6 × 600m with 3min recovery.

RUN SESSION 14

Session objective: Continuous alternate miles

Aim: To improve strength and be aware of pace judgement.

When to use: Off season and pre-season.

Description
Continuous 6- (or 8-) mile run, alternating between hard/easy/medium/hard/easy/medium. For this session, it is critical to know your race pace, particularly for 10km. For example, if a 5min 10sec mile pace was the overall pace/time (32.40) for 10km, the goal pace for hard/easy/medium would be: 5:10/6:10/5:40, with easy pace 1min per mile slower, and medium pace in between the two. Pace judgement is the absolute key in this session.

In shorthand: As above; Continuous 6- (or 8-) mile run alternating between hard/easy/medium/hard/easy/medium

Variations
For sprint-distance triathletes, change pace every 800m/half-mile for a total distance of 3 or 4 miles. Beginners over the Olympic distance should also start here.

The ability to accelerate away from a pack when running is something that can be practised during training.

RUN SESSION 15

Session objective: Repetition 200m

Aim: To build and improve endurance and strength endurance.

When to use: Off season and pre-season; occasionally during the season if endurance is felt to be slipping away.

Description
An old-fashioned interval session that is the bread-and-butter staple diet of most middle- and long-distance runners and triathletes. Twenty (say) repetitions of 200m are run (track is good for this), with a jog across recovery from finish to start line. The pace should be faster than race pace, so effectively best 3km pace or faster. Around 6,000m is covered during the session, as well as warm-up and warm-down.

In shorthand: 20 × 200m, jog across recovery

Variations
Lots! Increase the number of repetitions, decrease or increase the recovery (interval) phase with regard to level of fitness. I well remember running two sets of 30 × 200m in my (long distant!) competitive days.

RUN SESSION 16

Session objective: Tempo and plus-tempo pace run

Aim: To step up from race pace/tempo speed, and maintain this to the end of the session/race. This session is also hugely significant for the athlete's mental attitude.

When to use: Pre-season, early season, occasionally during the season if you have a long gap between races.

Description
- 12min run, gradually increase pace to 'hard' for final 4min, then...
- 2min jog, then...
- 5 × 400m hard with 200m jog (or, 90sec hard with 60sec jog),
- one further minute jog, then back to...
- 12min run, hard as possible throughout.

In shorthand: 12min; 5 × 400m (200m recovery) 12min hard

Variations
For sprint distance, drop to 6min at start and finish, and 6 × 200m in the mid-section.

Getting into a good position for the start of the run discipline is important.

RUN SESSION 17

Session objective: Maintenance of pace after initial effort at start of run discipline

Aim: To maintain race tempo when under pressure from a fast start.

When to use: Pre-season and early season.

Description
After warm up:

- 1min very hard
- 1min jog, then
- 6min at AT threshold,
- 3min steady jog
- Repeat twice more

In shorthand: 1 hard (recovery 1), 6 race pace plus (recovery 3) × 3

Pushing the pace hard from the start of the run will trim down the field immediately.

RUN SESSION 18

Session objective: Speed, increasing demand on endurance

Aim: To improve speed under pressure and to develop mental toughness.

When to use: During the season to sharpen; do not overuse this session!

Description

A very hard session that is particularly valuable for sprint-distance triathletes, but also very effective in developing speed endurance under pressure. The session is based at better than 1,500m best pace, even better if aimed at 800m racing pace!

- 200m is run at that pace, followed by...
- 30sec standing recovery only; then...
- 400m at the same pace again, with just a
- 30sec recovery.
- Finally a 600m effort at that pace.

For many triathletes that will be sufficient; some experienced triathletes may want to go through the set again, but after a 15min walk/jog recovery.

In shorthand: 200m, 400m, 600m, 30sec recovery

Variations

As above, repeat once more.

RUN SESSION 19

Session objective: Speed and leg speed and cadence

When to use: Pre-season and during race season.

Description

The basic single most important aspect in determining pure speed is how fast your legs turn over (mobility and leg length are also, of course, important). We aim to increase speed and leg cadence as this session progresses.

- Four sets of 1min at 10km race pace, with a 1min jog/recovery interval in between.
- Then take an easy 5min jog recovery.
- A further four sets of 1min, but this time at 5km race pace, with a 1min jog/recovery interval in between.
- Then take an easy 5min jog recovery.
- Finally, run four sets of 30sec at 99 per cent flat-out pace, with 60 to 90sec jog recovery.

In shorthand:

4 × 60sec @ 10km pace; 4 × 60sec @ 5km pace; 4 × 30sec @ 99 per cent; 60sec recovery, 5min between sets. Extra recovery on flat-out section

Variations

Do not increase the period of efforts, perhaps increase recovery if needed and if basic speed is low.

RUN SESSION 20

Session objective: Interval plus sustained effort

Aim: To improve Ironman® and half Ironman® speed.

When to use: All year.

This session has been used by Ironman® women's World Champion Chrissie Wellington amongst others. After the warm-up, 800m is run at 3km/5km pace with a 200m jog as the resting interval; this is repeated fifteen times. Immediately after the fifteenth repetition, the athlete goes into a hard 3-mile run, finishing with a final 800m uphill.

Description
- 15 × 800m at 3km/5km pace
- 200m jog recovery, then to a
- 3-mile hard run.

The rationale behind this session makes sense. The total distance is approximately 13 miles (a half-marathon), with substantially more than half the distance at faster than half-marathon pace. It is an entirely appropriate session for distance triathletes.

Variations
- 10 × 600m (200m jog recovery) at 1,500m/3km pace into a hard 3km run for experienced Olympic-distance athletes.
- Extend repetition distance to 1,000m for experienced Ironman® triathletes.

RUN SESSION 21

Session objective: The long run

Aim: To build endurance and stamina.

When to use: Always predominantly off season, and also pre-season, but still necessary during the racing season to maintain stamina.

Description
Whatever your racing distance, whether it is sprint, Olympic, half Ironman® or Ironman®, the long run is a crucial and essential part of training. The initial starting point should be just to run, without worrying about speed or pace. The long run not only builds endurance, it also teaches the body to utilize fat as a fuel, and is a strong part of mental training and conditioning.

How long is a long run? The easy answer is that a long run is any distance further than your racing distance (Ironman® athletes, don't panic! Different rules apply for you…) – so, more than 5km, 10km, 20km would be a long run for the race distances of sprint, Olympic and half Ironman®. How far is the longest we should run? I would suggest around twice the racing distance, although sprint-distance athletes might want to lengthen this, half Ironman® competitors to shorten it.

Variations
As above for the four racing distances, however there are several variations of the long run that we should treat as separate sessions, rather than variations. One that we can include here is easy.

At the end of the long run, take 2min very easy jog recovery, and then go into four sets of 80 to 100m fast leg-turnover strides to get that 'speed' feeling back into the legs using the fast-twitch muscles.

RUN SESSION 22

Session objective: The long run, out and back version

Aim: As well as building endurance and stamina, this is an excellent session to teach the body to run fast when tired.

When to use: This session always seems to be particularly effective pre-season, but use during the race season if there is a significant time gap between races.

Description
An excellent session, particularly for full and half Ironman® distance:

- Run out 10km (6 miles) steady.
- Take 2min recovery, and…
- run back, aiming to negative split ie return faster than the outward run.

In shorthand: 2 × 10km, + 2min

Variations
This session can be used effectively for Olympic-distance training by simply halving the distance: run out for 5km, and return the same 5km with a negative split.

RUN SESSION 23

Session objective: The long run, increasing demand

Aim: As the previous session, as well as building endurance and stamina, this is an excellent session to teach the body to run fast when tired.

When to use: Again, this session seems to be particularly effective pre-season. And again, use during the race season if there is a significant time gap between races.

Description
Another session that works particularly well for full and half Ironman® distance:

* Run for 15min at easy to steady, straight into…
* the next 15min at steady to hard, then finally into…
* 1hr at race pace, or race pace plus.

In shorthand: 15 + 15 + 60

Variations
* 15min steady, into 15min at increased pace, into 15min at race pace plus; then repeat straight back into 15min steady, fast, race pace.
* This session can be used effectively for Olympic-distance training by simply halving the distance: run out for 5km and return the same 5km with a negative split.

RUN SESSION 24

Session objective: The long run at race pace

When you have finished your first Ironman® or half Ironman®, the target becomes not just finishing, but the time that you finish in. Set out your target time. Base it on your finishing time for your first half or full Ironman®, but also use the 'pure' running times over marathon, half-marathon and 10km; thus:

6min miles = half-marathon time of 1 hr 18min
7min miles = half-marathon time of 1hr 31min
8min miles = half-marathon time of 1hr 45min
9min miles = half-marathon time of 1hr 58min
10min miles half-marathon time of 2hr 11min.

Double these times for full Ironman® /marathon.

Aim: To improve significantly on (particularly) half and full Ironman® race times.

When to use: Off season and pre-season.

Description

Step one for this 'target' training is to begin with just over one third of the half or full marathon distance, 5 miles and 9 miles respectively, and run this distance at your target speed: 30, 35, 40, 45, or 50min for half-marathon; and 54, 63, 72, 81 or 90min for full marathon respectively.

During the initial starting phase of training, run this 5- or 9-mile distance once a week until you can hit this target speed, not once but for two weeks in succession. This will minimize the chance of a 'freak' week. When you have run the two sets of 5 or 9 miles, it is time to move up just 1 mile in distance to 6 miles or 10 miles and maintain that pace, now giving us 6-mile times of 36, 42, 48, 54, 60min, and 10-mile times of 60, 70, 80, 90 and 100min respectively.

This single aspect of training should be continued up to runs of around 10 miles and 18 miles, two-thirds of half and full marathon distance. Do not assume that progression will be consistent and constant: there will be hiccups and plateaus when no improvement seems to be made for some time, and then there will be a big step forwards.

In shorthand: Distance pace running

Variations
Not for this.

RUN SESSION 25

Session objective: Hill repetitions

Aim: To improve strength and maintain speed on hills.

When to use: Always, particularly pre-season.

Description
A series of hill repetitions with a jog down recovery.

It is important to maintain good technique in this session in order to be able to replicate that during races. The popular cliché (emanating from the Kenyan running camp) is that if there were only one type of running training available, then hills are the best. The session should be a mixture of endurance, strength and speed. However, too long a session will be detrimental to maintaining a good technique.

Hills should not be too steep or technique will suffer, nor too long for the same reason.

Start with a possible eight repetitions of around 30sec, and gradually increase to sixteen.

In shorthand: 8 × 30sec hills, jog down recovery

Variations
As above, gradually increase the number of repetitions. For beginners perhaps start with 20sec rather than 30; for more quality and speed, increase recovery.

RUN SESSION 26

Session objective: Maintaining speed after hill repetitions

Aim: To improve strength and maintain speed on and after hills.

When to use: Always, particularly pre-season.

Description
A series of hill repetitions with a jog back and down recovery. However, after running uphill as in the previous session, the runner continues for another 30sec on the flat, holding the same speed.

Again, the session is a mixture of endurance, strength and speed.

The rationale behind this is that many runners are conditioned to work hard on hills, but then ease back (perhaps unconsciously) when the hill run is completed.

Start with a possible five repetitions of around 30sec up and 30sec flat, and gradually increase to ten.

In shorthand: 8 × 30 + 30sec hills plus flat, jog back and down recovery.

Variations
As above, gradually increase number of repetitions. For beginners perhaps start with 20sec rather than 30 on both uphill and flat. For more quality and speed, increase recovery.

RUN SESSION 27

Session objective: Maintaining speed for hilly courses (zig-zag hills)

Aim: To improve strength and maintain speed on and after hills, and to combat cumulative fatigue and demand.

When to use: Always, particularly pre-season.

Description
A series of combined hill repetitions. A very tough session! We start with running uphill as in the previous session, then at the top of the hill the runner turns and runs down, at the bottom turn once again and run back up. If the uphill run is 30sec, this one repetition is 90sec.

Again, the session is a mixture of endurance, strength and speed, and also pure guts and determination. The rationale behind this is that the effect of running hilly courses is cumulative, and putting together two hills in a single repetition will condition the athlete to being able to deal with this situation in a race.

This session is intense and will require adequate recovery.

Start with three repetitions only, gradually increase to eight.

In shorthand: 3 × 30/30/30sec up/down/up flat, take at least 90sec recovery in between repetitions

Variations
As above, gradually increase the number of repetitions. For beginners perhaps start with 20sec on each section.

RUN SESSION 28

Session objective: Hill repetitions from flat run

Aim: To improve strength and maintain speed on hills.

When to use: Always, particularly pre-season.

Description
A series of hill repetitions with a jog down recovery is covered, but this time with a hard flat run of around 30sec leading directly into the hill run. Maintaining speed on the hill after running hard into it will simulate race conditions and ensure that the hill effort is hard. Once again, the session should be a mixture of endurance, strength and speed.

Start with a possible six repetitions of around 30sec each of flat and hill, and gradually increase to twelve or more.

In shorthand: 6 × 30/30 flat into hill, jog back recovery

Variations
As above, gradually increase number of repetitions. For beginners perhaps start with 20sec rather than 30. For more quality and speed, increase recovery.

RUN SESSION 29

Session objective: Hill repetitions plus tempo

Aim: To improve strength and maintain speed on hills, and to simulate race pace conditions.

When to use: Always, particularly pre-season.

Description
A series of hill repetitions with a jog down recovery is covered, with the addition of a 20min tempo run immediately after the final repetition. The cumulative effect of the hill repetitions will ensure that the effort required to maintain a sustained speed for the tempo run will be extremely hard and will resemble hard racing conditions.

Once again, the session is a mixture of endurance, strength and race pace speed.

Start with a possible eight repetitions of around 30sec each, and gradually increase to twelve or more before the flat tempo run.

In shorthand: 8 × 30 hills, jog back recovery > 20min tempo run

Variations
- As above, gradually increase number of repetitions. For beginners perhaps start with 20sec rather than 30.
- Beginners should perhaps start with a 10min tempo run, experienced triathletes and half/Ironman® competitors can increase to 1hr.

RUN SESSION 30

Session objective: To improve technique

While swimming in particular has a strong emphasis on technique work, running often has little. This is rationalized by the assumption 'Well, everybody can run!': yes they can, but not always well. Work on technique is never wasted.

Aim: To emphasize good running technique.

When to use: Always.

Description
Refer back to the running technique chapter; choose several aspects of technique (not too many) and work on these for between 30 and 60m. Take a jog or walk back after each effort. Continue for between twenty and sixty repetitions.

In shorthand: 20–60 × 30–60m tech reps (walk/jog back recovery)

Variations
Aspects of technique, number of repetitions, distance of each repetition, recovery.

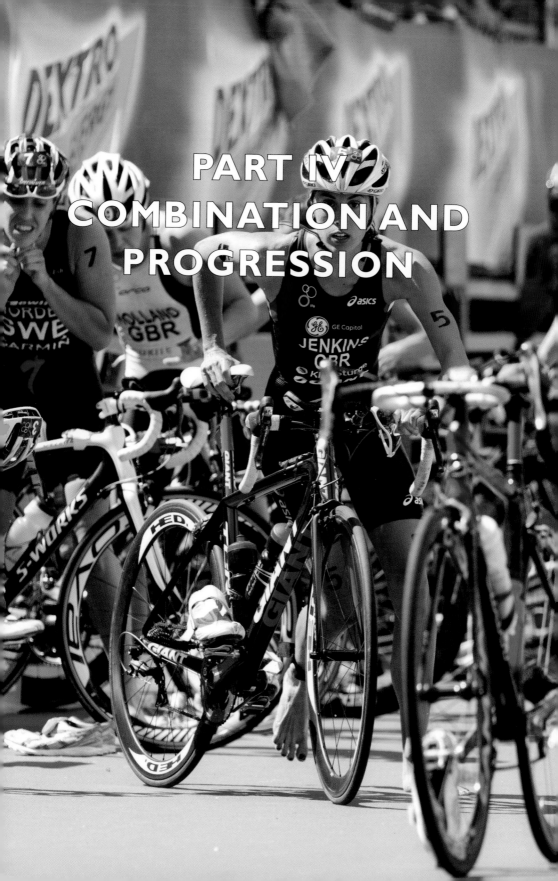

PART IV
COMBINATION AND
PROGRESSION

CHAPTER 8

THE BRICK SESSIONS

The very essence of the sport of triathlon is the combination of the three disciplines and how well (or badly) the athlete's body can deal with it. It makes total sense that somebody who is prepared for a hard run immediately after a hard bike section will run faster. Therefore it is essential to prepare for this transition by simulating it in training sessions.

However, brick sessions are hard and demanding: they should be used with caution, and adequate recovery should be allowed after them. As with any single discipline session, the schedule should take into account the number of low-key and intensive sessions, and those that are short in duration and those that are time-consuming.

How well you recover from a brick session is – as with single discipline training sessions – a very individual process. However, in general brick sessions are more demanding and do need more recovery time.

Brick session 1: Olympic distance up to Ironman®

Brick session 2: Olympic distance up to Ironman®

Brick session 3: Cycle hills

Brick session 4: Cycle flat time trial

Brick session 5: Double run

Brick session 6: Cycle to run

Brick session 7: Swim to cycle

Brick session 8: Speed-endurance bike to run

Brick session 9: Swim

Brick session 10: Mini triathlon

BRICK SESSION 1

Session objective: Bricks for Olympic distance up to Ironman®

The classic brick session for triathletes is a cycle followed by a run, the distances of each varying with the overall racing distance, and the age, experience and standard of the athlete. It is a very basic session, and although necessary, should not be used too much, nor as the only brick or back-to-back session.

Aim: To improve the ability to run well off the bike, and to be able to maintain running technique.

When to use: Mainly off season, and sometimes (with caution) pre-season.

Description
Classic Olympic distance, between 10- and 25-mile cycle, followed by between 3- and 6-mile run. For half Ironman® and Ironman® the distances go up, of course, perhaps as much as an 80-mile cycle followed by a half-marathon run for full distance Ironman®.

Variations
As above, vary the distances.

Brick and transition training mean that you will have swift changeovers during races.

BRICK SESSION 2

Session objective: Bricks for Olympic distance up to Ironman® (complex)

As described in the first session, the classic brick session for Olympic-distance/Ironman® athletes is a long cycle followed by a long run, the distances of each varying with the total racing distance, and the age, experience and standard of the athlete. There is sometimes concern that too much of this type of session can actually detract from efficient running off the bike.

Aim: To improve running speed and technique off the bike.

When to use: Mainly off season, and sometimes (with caution) pre-season.

Description
For Ironman®/half Ironman®:
40min cycle (road or turbo) into a 20min run, going through three times, so
40min cycle > 20min run >
40min cycle > 20min run >
40min cycle > 20min run

For Olympic distance athletes:
20 to 30min cycle > 10 to 20min run >
20 to 30min cycle > 10 to 20min run >
20 to 30min cycle > 10 to 20min run

Variations
- Two repetitions only.
- Drop cycle time to 15min, drop run time to 5min only.

BRICK SESSION 3

Session objective: Cycle hills

Aim: To achieve high cadence and good technique, in order to run fast off the bike when the legs are heavy.

When to use: All year, but particularly pre-season.

Description
- Warm up, then…
- Hill climb, 5km cycle for 800m/3min…
- Descend and repeat ten times in all.
- Immediately after the final cycle repetition, transition into 20min run.

Variations
- Number of repetitions.
- Length and severity of climbs.

The mass exit from transition must be worked on during training.

BRICK SESSION 4

Session objective: Cycle a flat time trial

In effect we are reversing the previous session. This is a great session for adjusting your 'running' legs to a race with a severe run or start to the run discipline.

Aim: To run strongly off a fast pace bike.

When to use: All year, but particularly pre-season.

Description
- Warm up, then…
- cycle a flat time trial, 15 to 20 miles (or around two thirds of the race distance), and…
- from transition immediately into…
- 10 × 60 to 90sec hill repetitions,
- jog down for recovery each time.

Variations
- Number of repetitions.
- Length and severity of climbs.

BRICK SESSION 5

Session objective: Double run day

In the morning, run a long distance: if preparing for Ironman®, this can be up to 20 miles. In the late afternoon run again, but this time between 3 and 6 miles.

Aim: To achieve high cadence and good technique. To teach the body that it can run when very fatigued and after minimal nutrition.

When to use: Pre-race. It is suggested around six weeks before the race.

Description
Although we are not combining a cycle/run or swim/cycle in this session, I still think it should be classified as a brick/back to back. It is particularly effective for longer distance events, including Ironman®.

- Run long in the morning: 2hr, 20 miles.
- Don't eat after the run, but rather take in fluid either as water or fruit juice.
- Between 5 to 7hr after completing the long run, run again between 20 and 45min.

Variations
- For a half Ironman®, cut down the length of the runs to 10 miles and 4 miles. The pace would be faster than in a preparation for a full Ironman®.
- For an Olympic distance, run 6 miles in the morning and 3 miles fast in the afternoon.

BRICK SESSION 6

Session objective: Cycle to run

In this session you cycle 5km and follow it immediately with a 1,000m run, five times, each one faster than the previous one. Adjust the repetition times for the run: this example is aimed at a 37.30 10km pace athlete.

Aim: To run fast off the bike when you're tired. The session has a fairly obvious philosophy of running faster each time when you're that little bit more tired each time from the preceding effort. It's a tough old session, but one that works...

When to use: All year, but particularly pre-season.

Description
Warm up, then...

- 5km cycle in 7½ to 8min, then a fast transition immediately into...
- 1,000m run in 3min 45sec (37.30 10km pace), then...
- rest between 3 to 5min.

- Repeat 5km cycle in 7½ to 8min, then...
- 1,000m run in 3min 35sec (36.30 10km pace), then...
- rest between 3 to 5min.

- Repeat 5km cycle in 7½ to 8min, then...
- 1,000m run in 3min 25sec (35.30 10km pace), then...
- rest between 3 to 5min.

- Repeat 5km cycle in 7½ to 8min, then...
- 1,000m run in 3min 15sec (34.30 10km pace), then...
- rest between 3 to 5min.

- Repeat 5km cycle in 7½ to 8min, then...
- 1,000m run in between 3min to 3.05sec (33 to 33.30 10km pace).

Variations
- No rest in between efforts during the off season to make more of an endurance/ aerobic session.
- Cut down to three repetitions with increased recovery in between for a taper session immediately before an important race.

BRICK SESSION 7

Session objective: Swim-to-cycle training

It's surprising how many triathletes will focus on their bike-to-run training, yet never do a swim-to-bike.

Aim: To practise transition, to cycle hard after a swim, and to simulate race conditions safely.

When to use: All year, but particularly pre-season.

Description
If possible, get permission to set up a turbo trainer on poolside or in the changing rooms.

- Swim 400m
- Exit pool, run to bike/turbo, change into racing cycle kit...
- Cycle 15min

Variations
- Repeat session, as in swim/cycle/swim/cycle.
- Vary the distances, as in 600m, 800m swim; 10, 12, 20min cycle.

BRICK SESSION 8

Session objective: Speed-endurance bike to run

Aim: To practise transition; to run hard and fast after a hard and fast cycle; to simulate race conditions safely.

When to use: All year, but particularly pre-season.

Description
Best carried out on a running track; set up your own transition zone, as you would for a race; then…

- cycle 800m (two laps of the track) flat out; then…
- into transition…
- change into bike kit and shoes…
- run 400m flat out.

Repeat four times through in total.

Variations
- Vary the number of repetitions.
- Vary the distances of cycle and run: 1,200m, 1,600m cycle; 800m run

Transition training plays a huge part in being able to run fast off a tough bike ride.

BRICK SESSION 9

Session objective: Swim

This may not appear to be a back-to-back/brick session immediately, as it is all water-based. However, the strong use of legs/kicking ensures the brick effect, simulating the stages of an open-water multi-loop race.

Aim: To simulate tired legs, but only using swimming.

When to use: All year, but particularly pre-season.

Description
Ideally this should be performed as a group, but it can also work as an individual session.

Warm-up:
- 200 FC, 50 choice drills, 200 FC, 50 pull no float, 200 FC, 50 kick no float (extension position), 50 easy.

Subset:
This set gets the HR up and recreates a race start. Minimal rest before the main set.

- Teams of three, two teams per lane, twenty-four people in a six-lane pool.
- As a relay, swimmers build hard single lengths and exit, handing over to team-mates.
- Each team of three races to get twenty-four lengths swum as a team.

Main set:
After the subset 'start' swimmers relax into a cruise swim. Then spike the HR with a strong leg section (imagine a multi-loop course where you exit and return to the water). Practising returning to 'cruise' after the HR spike is an essential skill.

- 600 FC pull (no paddles, just pull buoy) at 70 per cent; rest 30.
- 2 × IL hard kick with a board or use breaststroke arms, or aquajog if pool is deep enough; rest 30sec.
- 400 FC swim with paddles at 75 per cent; rest 30sec.
- 2 × IL hard kick with a board, or use breaststroke arms, or aquajog if pool is deep enough; rest 30sec.
- 600 FC swim at 80 per cent; rest 30sec.
- 2 × IL hard kick with a board, or use breaststroke arms...
- Finish strongly to simulate the 'running exit' to T1.

BRICK SESSION 9 (*continued*)

Recall that a good kick means toes pointed backwards to the wall you have pushed off from, not at the bottom of the pool. Legs predominantly straight, kick originating in the hip, not the knee.

Swim-down:
200m cool down, your choice at 40 per cent effort.

Total yardage: Between 2,650 and 4,200m.

Variations
- The 200s can be swum as 100s if pushed for time.
- On your own: 12 × 25m, half-length sprint from a treading water position. No touching any wall at any point.
- Number of repetitions.

BRICK SESSION 10

Session objective: Mini triathlon

This session consists of a mini triathlon done at race speed, preferably at the race site or in similar conditions, with suitable pre-race preparation.

Aim: Race preparation and simulation.

When to use: In the race season, and sometimes pre-season.

Description
200m swim, 5km bike, 1km run.

All this session should be done at full effort, if at all possible on the racecourse using the race transition area. Particular attention and hard work should be given to going in and out of the transition as well as through it.

Variations
Go through twice, after taking advice from a coach or another athlete who has observed you.

There is frequently a necessity to sprint to move away from a run pack.

CHAPTER 9

PROGRESSION IN TRAINING

Whatever your starting point in training, you can't afford to stay there if you want to make progress, to get faster and to race better. It is therefore essential to make training harder and more challenging.

Simple progression in training can be as follows (these are examples only):

- Continuous running/cycling/swimming for a longer time
- Training for the same time but at a higher speed
- Lifting heavier weights
- Doing the same amount of work in a shorter time
- Reducing recovery time between efforts
- Increasing the time of efforts/repetitions
- Increasing the number of repetitions
- Increasing resistance:
    in running, hills;
    in cycling, bigger gears;
    in swimming, adding paddles and drag costumes.

There many ways to progress in training and still keep the sessions interesting and fun. One way of looking at it is to 'think dirty':

We have made frequent reference in the descriptions of training sessions to the variations we can use during the sessions. In relation to that, it is important that we don't just do the same sessions time and time again, but that we progress these sessions. Progressions can be made in terms of time, speed, effort, distance, recoveries and, of course, combinations of these.

In this chaper we offer two examples of progressive sessions, one for running, and one for turbo training on the bike. They are just examples, and the triathlete should decide their own starting point on these types of session, and the overall timescale to make the progressions. A realistic timescale for the improvements/progression shown here might be around six months.

THINK DIRTY!

DISTANCE

INTERVAL

REPETITION

TIME

YOU

During the early stages of the run, pace judgement is crucial.

A Starting Schedule for Progression in Running Training

Let us start with a fairly simple training session, namely four repetitions of one mile to be completed in 6min each, with a resting interval of 4min between each repetition.

Distance: 1 mile
Interval: 4min
Repetition: 3 reps
Time: 6min

The test can be improved/made harder by increasing or reducing the number of any of the factors involved – thus we can:

- increase the number of repetitions
- increase the distance of the repetitions
- decrease the resting time between the repetitions
- decrease the time taken for completing the repetitions

First increase:
Distance 1 mile, interval 4min rest, repetition 4 reps, time 6min.

First decrease:
Distance 1 mile, interval 3min rest, repetition 4 reps, time 6min.

Second decrease:
Distance 1 mile, interval 3min rest, repetition 4 reps, time 5min 40sec.

Second increase
Distance 2,000m, interval 3min rest, repetition 4 reps, time 7min 5sec (the pace for each 400m is 5sec faster).

A Starting Schedule for Progression in Cycling Training

There is no reason why the turbo sessions in the example given below should not be done on the road. However, the practicalities of real life mean that turbo training can be monitored more easily and is safer. The figures '52' and '42' refer to the number of teeth on the outer and inner chainring; the other numbers – 22, 20, 18, 16, 15, 14 and 13 – refer to the number of teeth on the rear gear sprockets: the lower the number, the harder (bigger) the gear.

STAGE 1 (introductory)
Session 1
5 reps of 52 × 20 for 1min, aim for 100 rpm
Recovery: 42 × 20 for 1min at 60 rpm

Session 2
7 reps of 52 × 20 for 1min, aim for 100 rpm
Recovery: 42 × 20 for 1min at 60 rpm

Session 3
10 reps of 52 × 20 for 1min, aim for 100 rpm
Recovery: 42 × 20 for 1min at 60 rpm

Session 4
5 reps of 52 × 20 for 2min, aim for 100 rpm
Recovery: 42 × 20 for 1min at 60 rpm

STAGE 2
Session 1
5 reps of 52 × 18 for 2min, aim for 100 rpm
Recovery: 42 × 18 for 1min at 60 rpm

Session 2
10 reps of 52 × 18 for 1min, aim for 100 rpm
Recovery: 42 × 18 for 1min at 60 rpm

Session 3
7 reps of 52 × 18 for 2min, aim for 100 rpm
Recovery: 42 × 18 for 1min at 60 rpm

Session 4
5 reps of 52 × 20 for 3min, aim for 100 rpm
Recovery: 42 × 20 for 1min at 60 rpm

STAGE 3
Session 1
7 reps of 52 × 16 for 2min, aim for 100 rpm
Recovery: 42 × 16 for 1min at 60 rpm

Session 2
15 reps of 52 × 18 for 1min, aim for
100 rpm
Recovery: 42 × 18 for 1min at 60 rpm

Session 3
4 reps of 52 × 20 for 2min, aim for 100 rpm,
straight into:
52 × 18 for 2min, aim for 100 rpm
Recovery: 42 × 20 for 1min at 60 rpm after
each 4min effort

Session 4
3 reps of 52 × 20 for 2min, aim for 100 rpm,
straight into:
52 × 18 for 2min, aim for 100 rpm, straight
into:
52 × 16 for 1min, aim for 100 rpm
Recovery: 42 × 20 for 1min at 60 rpm after
each 5min effort

STAGE 4
Session 1
3 reps of 52 × 18 for 3min, aim for 100 rpm,
straight into:
52 × 16 for 2min, aim for 100 rpm, straight
into:
52 × 15 for 1min, aim for 100 rpm
Recovery: 42 × 20 for 1min at 60 rpm after
each 6min effort

Session 2
12 reps of 52 × 16 for 1min, aim for
100 rpm
Recovery: 52 × 22 for 1min at 60 rpm

Session 3
3 reps of: 52 × 20 for 4min, aim for
100 rpm, straight into:
52 × 18 for 3min, aim for 100 rpm, straight
into:
52 × 16 for 2min, aim for 100 rpm
Recovery: 42 × 20 for 1min at 60 rpm after
each 9min effort

Session 4
10 reps of 52 × 18 for 2min, aim for
100 rpm
Recovery: 42 × 18 for 1min at 60 rpm

STAGE 5
Session 1
2 reps of 52 × 22 for 2min, aim for 100 rpm,
straight into:
52 × 20 for 2min, aim for 100 rpm, straight
into:
52 × 18 for 2min, aim for 100 rpm, straight
into:
52 × 16 for 2min, aim for 100 rpm, straight
into:
52 × 15 for 2min, aim for 100 rpm, straight
into:
52 × 14 for 2min, aim for 100 rpm, straight
into:
Recovery: 42 × 22 for 2min at 60 rpm after
first set of 12min effort

Session 2
15 reps of 52 × 16 for 1min, aim for 100 rpm
Recovery: 52 × 22 for 1min at 60 rpm

Session 3
3 reps of 52 × 20 for 3min, aim for 100 rpm,
straight into:
52 × 18 for 3min, aim for 100 rpm, straight
into:
52 × 16 for 3min, aim for 100 rpm, straight
into:
Recovery: 42 × 22 for 2min at 60 rpm after
each set of 9min effort

Session 4
8 reps of 52 × 16 for 2min, aim for 100 rpm
Recovery: 52 × 22 for 1min at 60 rpm

STAGE 6
Session 1
1 rep of 52 × 20 for 4min, aim for 100 rpm
Recovery: 52 × 22 for 1min at 60 rpm

1 rep for 52 × 18 for 4min, aim for 100 rpm
Recovery: 52 × 22 for 1min at 60 rpm

1 rep of 52 × 17 for 4min, aim for 100 rpm
Recovery: 52 × 22 for 1min at 60 rpm

1 rep of 52 × 16 for 4min, aim for 100 rpm
Recovery: 52 × 22 for 1min at 60 rpm

1 rep of 52 × 15 for 4min, aim for 100 rpm
Recovery: 52 × 22 for 1min at 60 rpm

1 rep of 52 × 14 for 4min, aim for
100 rpm
Recovery: 52 × 22 for 1min at 60 rpm

Session 2
15 reps of 52 × 15 for 1min, aim for
100 rpm
Recovery: 52 × 22 for 1min at 60 rpm

Session 3
3 reps of: 52 × 17 for 4min, aim for
100 rpm, straight into:
52 × 16 for 4min, aim for 100 rpm, straight
into:
52 × 15 for 4min, aim for 100 rpm
Recovery: 52 × 22 for 2min at 60 rpm after
each set of 12min

Session 4
8 reps of 52 × 15 for 2min, aim for
100 rpm
Recovery: 52 × 22 for 1min at 60 rpm

STAGE 7
Session 1
1 rep of 52 × 18 for 8min, aim for 100 rpm
Recovery: 52 × 22 for 2min at 60 rpm

1 rep of 52 × 17 for 8min, aim for 100 rpm
Recovery: 52 × 22 for 2min at 60 rpm

1 rep of 52 × 16 for 8min, aim for 100 rpm
Recovery: 52 × 22 for 2min at 60 rpm

1 rep of 52 × 15 for 8min, aim for 100 rpm
Recovery: 52 × 22 for 2min at 60 rpm

1 rep of 52 × 14 for 8min, aim for 100 rpm
Recovery: 52 × 22 for 2min at 60 rpm

Session 2
15 reps of 52 × 14 for 1min, aim for 100 rpm
Recovery: 52 × 22 for 1min at 60 rpm

Session 3
3 reps of 52 × 17 for 6min, aim for 100 rpm,
straight into:
52 × 16 for 6min, aim for 100 rpm, straight
into:
52 × 15 for 6min, aim for 100 rpm
Recovery: 52 × 22 for 2min at 60 rpm after
each set of 18min

Session 4
10 reps of 52 × 14 for 2min, aim for 100
rpm
Recovery: 52 × 22 for 1min at 60 rpm

Progression in Swimming Training

Similar examples apply to swimming, though one of the limiting factors is, of course, juggling the sessions to the length of the pool. However, target times can be reduced, and resting intervals can also be lowered.

INDEX